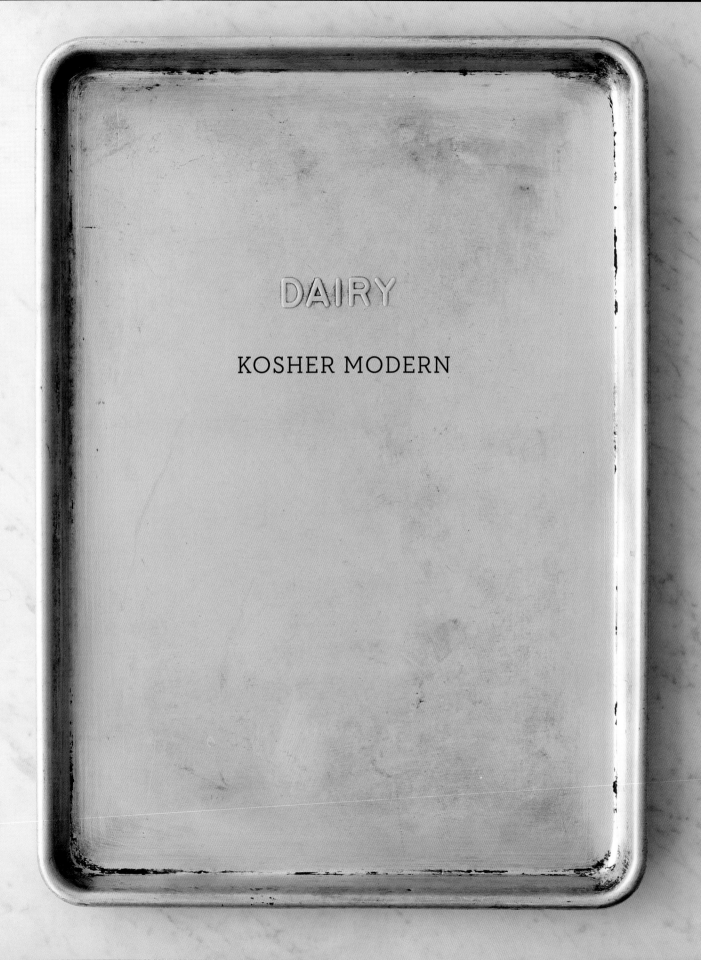

DAIRY

KOSHER MODERN

KOSHER MODERN

Gourmet World Recipes for the Kosher Cook

BY GEILA HOCHERMAN AND ARTHUR BOEHM

PHOTOGRAPHY BY ANTONIS ACHILLEOUS

KYLE BOOKS

For my daughter Tess and mother Allie, in memory of my grandmother Goldie and great-grandmother Tova, and for all the generations of women who have communicated love through their food.   GH

For Richard Getke, still the best dining partner, even at separate tables. AB

First published in Great Britain in 2011 by Kyle Books
23 Howland Street
London W1T 4AY
general.enquiries@kylebooks.com
www.kylebooks.com

ISBN: 978-0-857830-36-4

Text © 2011 by Geila Hocherman
Photographs © 2011 by Antonis Achilleous
Book design © 2011 by Kyle Cathie Ltd

Project editor: Anja Schmidt
Photographer: Antonis Achilleous
Food styling: Susan Vajaranant and Geila Hocherman
Copy editor: Helen Chin
Anglicisation: Lisa Morris
Production by Nic Jones, Sheila Smith and Lisa Pinnell

A CIP catalogue record for this title is available from the British Library

Colour reproduction by Scanhouse
Printed and bound in China

Contents

Foreword by Arthur Schwartz

Just as I was moving from my kitchen table to the computer to write this foreword, a wind came up and blew the loose galley pages of *Kosher Modern* onto the floor. My kitchen now paved with recipes for Miso-Glazed Black Cod; Ceviche with Avocado and Tortilla Chips; Chicken with Sausage, Fennel and Peas; Pistachio-Crusted Tuna with Wasabi Mayonnaise; and Cauliflower Paneer Masala, not to mention Bubbie's Brisket, I saw that this was truly a revolutionary book.

For a kosher cook, of the above list of dishes, which are typical of the whole book, only Bubbie's Brisket would have been both physically and psychically possible ten years ago. Where would I have found kosher miso for the cod? Who would have thought to marinate fish in lime juice and eat it 'raw'? In fact, it was only last year that I found Italian-style kosher sausage. Kosher wasabi for the trendy mayo may not be brand new, but in kosher time, it's close to being so. Kosher paneer, a kind of cheese, a salute to Indian and Pakistani cuisine? Well, you have to make that yourself – though it's easy following Geila Hocherman's instructions.

Jews have always eaten the food of the secular culture in which we live, adopting and adapting that cuisine to kosher dietary requirements, whether German, Polish, Russian, Hungarian, Romanian, French, Italian, Spanish, Middle Eastern of one kind or another, or what we used to think of as all-American. Nowadays, where I live, in Brooklyn, New York, pizza and sushi are by far the most popular kosher foods because they are by far the most popular secular foods.

Kosher is a set of rules, not a cuisine. Why shouldn't the kosher kitchen, encompass – nay, embrace – all the cuisines of the world, including the trendy chef-created food you see on television? Nowhere is it written that it shouldn't or can't. With Geila's 'tool box' system, and with so many exotic ingredients getting kosher certification, there's no excuse for kosher cooks not to turn out interesting, even sophisticated and, of course, very delicious meals every day and every holiday. *Kosher Modern* shows you how.

Getting Started

Introduction

I'm a kosher cook with a mission to make kosher cooking indistinguishable from any other kind. Don't get me wrong. I love good traditional kosher cooking – comforting, to be sure, but hardly 'gourmet'. I do it well, if I say so myself, and am always glad to add my versions of favourite recipes to the mix. You'll find some of them here. But my goal is to show you, whether you're a new cook or an old kitchen hand, how to make modern, blow-them-out-of-the-water kosher dishes – exciting, contemporary food – from wine-braised thin ribs to chicken satay with peanut sauce.

To do this, I offer an expanded culinary toolbox so you can make any dish you've seen and longed to try kosher, or convert dishes from, say, dairy to pareve with *nothing lost in translation*. Once you learn to recognise appropriate, best-tasting substitutes, you'll never have to settle for imitations of the 'real thing' again.

There are plenty of other advantages to 'kosher modern' cooking. Your cooking and menu making will benefit from an instant variety boost, which in turn will give increased pleasure you'll give to all those you cook for. Your understanding of cooking anatomy, of the techniques that define menu choices, will expand too, so you'll become a crack improviser, a creative kitchen force. And you'll gain flexibility – with your 'kosher modern' store cupboard, you'll comfortably serve six in an hour knowing, for example, that you can add mince or feta, chickpeas and beans to a stored ratatouille hash (see page 132) for a super chilli, fondly known in my house as Chilli Chillissimo.

Because I fell off the kosher wagon for a time, I know what *trafe* tastes like, and some of it is very, very good. So I can help you create the best, most diversely flavourful *kosher* cooking. While this book has only 95 recipes, it gives you access to every recipe there is. Once you see non-kosher recipes the way I do – as occasions for instant translation – you'll be able to cook kosher *anything*.

The Basics

We all know what makes kosher kosher. The dietary rules in a (kosher) nutshell are:

- Use kosher-certified ingredients only.
- All animals destined for the kosher table must be kosher-slaughtered and prepared.
- No shellfish, no pork.
- No dairy products served with meat.
- No fish and meat served on the same plate.

As in other areas of life, limitations can mean opportunities. It's all a matter of the way you think about what you want and how you go about getting it.

Your Menu Comes First

No dish stands alone. Each is part of a larger scheme – your menu. In cooking kosher, the choice of menu is particularly important, as meat and dairy dishes can't be served as part of the same meal. (Pareve dishes are, of course, a 'free pass'.) Therefore, what you make, and when it's made, will depend on your whole menu and when it's served.

Before turning on the hob I always ask myself a few questions. Some of these may seem basic to you, but they bear mentioning:

- What meal am I cooking for – breakfast, lunch or dinner?
- Is the meal for 'everyday' or for a special occasion, like a holiday? For the Shabbat or not?
- Will I be cooking for family or company?

Once you've answered these questions, ask yourself:

- What will I make? Will the dish be dairy, meat or pareve?
- What will I have to buy?
- What do I have on hand?

As regards bought versus stored items, it's important to strategise. I believe in the well-stocked freezer and store cupboard (see pages 17–19).

When constructing a menu, keep in mind that not every dish can or *should* be a star; your meal must be *orchestrated*. I like a big-impression opening dish, a solid main and a superb finish – a dessert to remember.

The important point is, for ease, versatility and best eating, always think menu first and make a plan.

Read Your Recipe

The inspiration for the *Kosher Modern* method began years ago, on the first day of classes I took at Le Cordon Bleu Paris. The professor said, '*Aujourd'hui nous faisons du porc à la bonne femme*' – 'Today we'll make pork braised with potatoes, onions and bacon.' I had a moment of panic but then I had a flash of inspiration: I could substitute veal for the pork.

When, later, we embarked on the preparation of a beef dish with a cream sauce, I had a similar epiphany: why not substitute salmon for the beef? This revelation led me to create my salmon with leeks braised in cream (page 69), a dish that's been the standout hit of many a dinner party.

The point is, when converting a recipe, you must first assess it. You'll want to know:

- which ingredients to change to ensure it's kosher;
- how to make certain the dish is *good* (assuming you'll have to substitute a 'high satisfaction' ingredient like butter for something else);
- when to regroup and create something entirely different.

Flavour and Ingredient Swapping

Finding the right ingredient exchanges is key to the 'kosher modern' approach. You want to maintain the fundamental character of the dish you'll be translating while ensuring its suitability for kosher dining. Your 'new' dish is bound to be different from the original, but that will be irrelevant once diners taste it.

For example, when I confront a shellfish recipe, I immediately think texture. My first choice is a firm-fleshed oily fish, one that won't fall apart in cooking and that provides something of the shellfish texture. My answer is sea bass or salmon. The chunky fish works beautifully when steamed or stewed, and is a chewy pleasure to eat. I also find that shellfish pungency can be duplicated by the addition of a strong fish stock. For the delicious result of such a conversion approach, see Bourride with Aioli, page 70.

Some translations are a cinch – for split-pea soup with chorizo, for example, all you'll need to do is substitute kosher chorizo for the ordinary kind. Others require more manipulation – for example, lasagne. I challenged myself to make this a dairy dish. I read my recipe, which of course included mince in the sauce. In place of the meat I used sliced mushrooms (first sautéing them to rid them of excess moisture and then, because of their stronger flavour, decreasing their amount relative to that of the meat). I also lightened the dish, replacing some of the original cheese with a light béchamel. The result on page 126 is more healthful than the original dish and every bit as satisfying.

The Subbing Rules of Thumb

- Look at the bigger picture. You must aim for ingredient parity. If you substitute milk in a recipe, you must also make up for lost fat and protein using, for example, a nut milk, which contains both. Exchanges must be delicious, but in addition to flavour, you must also consider food texture and temperature.

- Explore different cuisines, particularly those of Asian countries like China and India, which have a large vegetarian and low-dairy or no-dairy repertoire. Peruse vegan cookery books, whose special ingredients not only taste great but are good for you. Seeing how other cuisines and dietary disciplines handle ingredients will help you sub effectively and add new flavour notes to your cooking. You'll also increase your range.

- Expand your fat repertoire. Think nut oils – like walnut, for example. Margarine and vegetable shortening have been unjustly criticised, but both work just like butter in cooking and baking – enabling pastry flakiness, for example – and add no flavour of their own. That's a great opportunity to add flavour – say, cardamom or lemon in butterless almond crescent biscuits. Or pursue other options: my Macadamia Raspberry Tart (page 172), for example, has a crunchy all-nut crust.

- Translating recipes is, finally, about *learning*. The day I discovered I could make a fabulous buttercream using mostly Swiss meringue was a happy one. I even enjoy making mistakes so I can *learn* something. (However, I try not to experiment while cooking for guests.)

More About Texture

The basic dish elements are flavour and texture. Trying to translate texture when converting a dish can be problematic, especially when you need to thicken something – a soup, say – and your original recipe does so with 'dairy'.

Thickening often involves emulsification – the suspension of small droplets of one liquid in another. Emulsification is responsible for the texture of many sauces, such as hollandaise and vinaigrettes. Butter is also used with flour to make an emulsifying roux, or alone as a final body-making addition.

To get around the 'butter problem', ask yourself what will work like butter (or cream) to achieve an emulsion while contributing to, or not detracting from, best flavour. I've learned you can:

- Use oils by themselves to emulsify. Olive, basil or truffle oils help thicken while adding great flavour. Sometimes I combine olive oil with mashed roasted garlic that I've stored for a savoury thickener.

- Use egg yolks in place of cream.

- Make a roux with oil such as rapeseed or non-dairy fats. I've made terrific turkey gravy for Thanksgiving using the rendered fat from the turkey. Poultry fat also makes a great roux. (If you melt your own fresh chicken or duck fat, you get the bonus of gribenes – they're fabulous folded into mashed potatoes.)

- Thicken with ground mushrooms. You can use almost any kind – portobellos or porcini, if you can get them, are particularly good. If you want to make a dish that calls for meat and cheese, think mushrooms and cheese instead. You'll have something new, but better.

- Thicken with cooked puréed potatoes, onions, pulses and other vegetables.

Baking

There are three categories of kosher baking: dairy, pareve and Passover. Most of the world's sweet baked goods qualify as dairy. Pareve baking must be dairy-free and may require original-formula conversion. Passover baking must be wheat-free, as no wheat flour may be used (except, of course, in matzo making). No yeast may be used for Passover baking, but baking powder, bicarbonate of soda, potato starch and fine matzo meal are allowed – as, of course, are egg whites.

As with savoury dishes, you're aiming for baked goods with the flavour and texture of their non-kosher counterparts.

For pareve baking, subbing oils, margarine and shortening for butter are key. The rules are:

- Which fat you sub depends on what you're making. For biscuits that call for butter, as many do, I substitute margarine. The resulting crumb is better than if you use vegetable shortening. (You'll need to compensate for the lack of butter flavour by adding flavourings like lemon juice or spices such as cinnamon or cardamom.)

- For pastry cases, I use vegetable shortening, or shortening mixed with margarine. Like butter, vegetable shortening and margarine remain semi-solid when cut into flour, making flakiness, which depends on layerings of solid fat and flour, possible. Nut crusts, which are of course wheat-free, are the crusts of choice for Passover baking.

- For cakes, your options are butter, margarine or oil, depending on the crumb or cake style you're after. Pound cakes, for example, require butter, so you won't be serving these in a meat meal. For other cakes, you'll use margarine or oil (or no fat at all), depending on the cake's moisture 'profile', and/or the menu in which the cake will be served.

For pareve dessert making, I've also had wonderful results using nut milks in place of the animal kinds. Coconut milk and two relatively new kosher products – almond and hazelnut milk – are very useful in custards and pareve ice creams. Besides working like ordinary milk, they add special, subtle flavours of their own.

For Passover baking:

- Ground nuts – which contain protein and fat – can take the place of flour in cake making; they can also be used to make flourless pastry cases.

- Matzo meal, which is sold in different grades, fine being used for baking.

- Potato starch can be used in place of flour, but you must use it with matzo cake meal. Together they make a tenderer, better-tasting product than fine matzo meal used alone, which has a 'baked' flavour. Approximate proportions are: 225g of flour equals 170g of potato starch plus about 55g of fine matzo meal. See individual recipes and The Chart for exact proportions.

- Use baking powder, bicarbonate of soda and egg whites in the customary fashion for leavening.

Using this Book

At the head of each recipe you'll find one or more of the symbols M, D, P and PA. These stand for 'Meat', 'Dairy', 'Pareve' or 'Passover', indicating the dish type and, where applicable, possible variations. The first symbol after the title indicates the 'default' recipe version.

Convert It, which appears next to a recipe's method, is your guide to the ingredient exchanges that allow you to make, for example, a dairy or meat recipe pareve. Taken together, the Convert Its provide a distillation of 'modern' ingredient-exchange thinking. After reading a number of them, you should be able to make instant recipe conversions of your own.

The Chart, pages 198–201, is your reliable source of exchange info at a glance. It notes food items by type and by ingredient options (indicating, for example, milk substitutions, such as almond or soya milk, for making pareve dishes). The brand names that appear in it represent the best products I've found for making the tastiest, best-working exchanges. The Passover section is geared to baking and other dessert-making exchanges.

All of the ingredients are available online; see Sources, pages 202–203. Many can also be found in supermarkets, health food shops or Asian markets. When I first began cooking, the kosher store cupboard was almost bare. Now it's a cornucopia. Take advantage of it!

The Store Cupboard

Non-Dairy Milks and Cream

Almond and Hazelnut Milk. Made by blending nuts with water and then straining the result, these pareve milks are lower in fat and protein than their full-fat cow's milk equivalent. They're also low-cholesterol or cholesterol-free. Use them as you would dairy milks but note that they taste of the nut from which they've been made – and are often sweet, due to added sugars. I like to bake with them as their flavours really shine in cakes and other desserts. In savoury dishes they provide an additional flavour layer. I prefer Pacific Original nut milks, which have good flavour and texture, but the Ecomil brand is more readily available in the UK.

Coconut Milk. Ordinary coconut milk is made by steeping grated coconut in warm water or milk and then straining out the juice. Light coconut milk is prepared by diluting this liquid with water. It has about 60 per cent less fat than the ordinary kind, and a less creamy consistency. I use Blue Dragon brand for both types.

Soya Milk. Produced in Asia for millennia, soya milk is made by grinding cooked soybeans with water. It's higher in protein than cow's milk, but lower in fat and cholesterol-free. Most commercially available soya milks are clean tasting and add little flavour of their own. Look for non-sweetened varieties, like Alpro or Granovita.

Nut-Based Non-Dairy Cream. These nut-based products taste and work very much like cream. Unlike other non-dairy 'creamers', however, they have no waxy mouth-feel. I prefer MimicCreme Almond and Cashew Cream, which is unsweetened and remarkably like the real thing. For whipping, I use almond- and cashew-based MimicCreme Healthy Top. The Soyatoo brand is easier to find in the UK but it is not kosher-certified.

Oils and Fats

Margarine. This traditional vegetable-oil product works exactly like butter in baking and cooking, enabling, for example, flaky pastry cases and tender cakes. Because it has little flavour of its own, it invites the addition of dish-enhancing flavourings, like lemon or sweet spices. Kosher margarine is sold in a variety of forms. I use ordinary stick margarine only and recommend the Tomor brand.

Rendered Chicken Fat. Most kosher cooks are familiar with this time-honoured ingredient, which can be made at home – render chicken fat over the lowest possible heat, stirring, cool and refrigerate – or shop-bought, often from butchers. Similar to butter in its nutritional profile, it adds great flavour to many dishes, as well as providing body.

Rendered Duck Fat. A marvellous fat for frying or roasting potatoes, duck fat is more subtly flavoured than chicken fat, and is high in beneficial unsaturated fats. It also has a relatively high smoke point. Save fat scraps from kosher ducks to render yourself or buy it online, see Resources.

Toasted Sesame Seed Oil. A staple of the Chinese store cupboard, this thick, brownish oil, made from toasted sesame seeds, is for seasoning only. Don't confuse it with refined, almost flavourless sesame oils, which can be used for cooking. A brand I like is Mitoku.

White Truffle Oil. Made from olive oil, or a mixture of olive and other oils, this versatile ingredient is infused with white truffle, or contains white truffle flavouring. I use it to impart richness and earthy flavour to a variety of savoury dishes. It's especially good drizzled over finished dishes. D'Allasandro is my brand of choice.

Stocks and Broths

Chicken Stock. To make chicken stock for the recipes in this book, prepare Be-All, End-All Chicken Soup (page 54) without the beef ribs. Or use any high-quality kosher pareve stock, such as vegetable stock.

Imagine Organic No-Chicken Broth. Vegetable-based and pareve, this works remarkably well as a chicken (or vegetable) stock substitute.

G. Washington's Golden and Seasoning Broth. This pareve vegetable-based powder is another good chicken stock substitute, and may also be used without dilution as a seasoning in, for example, dips.

Seasonings and Condiments

Miso. A traditional Japanese ingredient that most commonly appears as the main ingredient of miso soup, miso is a savoury seasoning paste. It's made from rice, barley and/or soy beans. For the recipes in this book, I recommend rice-based shiro miso, also known as white miso, or soybean-based hatcho miso. The brand I use for both is Mitoku.

Mirin. This traditional Japanese rice wine with sugar adds a touch of sweetness to many dishes. I use it in marinades, dressings, sauces and as a seasoning. My preferred brand is Mitoku.

Soy Sauce. Used in China for more than 3,000 years, this essential Asian seasoning is made from soybeans, flour and water. It should be naturally brewed rather than chemically produced – look for 'naturally brewed' on labels. Pass by sauces that include hydrolysed soy protein, corn syrup and caramel colour, ingredients that denote synthetic sauce. Kikkoman is the brand I use most often.

Other Ingredients

Cheese. A vast array of 'authentic' kosher cheese is now available. Of the cheeses I recommend, a kosher version of Parmigiano-Reggiano, Italy's pre-eminent Parmesan, is produced by Pietro Fanticini, a third-generation cheese maker in Parmigiano-Reggiano territory. Gabriel Coulet, based in Roquefort-sur-Soulzon, produces authentic Roquefort with a heckscher. Kosher raclette, the semi-firm, Gruyère-like cow's milk cheese, is available from Fromages Ermitage, in Vosges and Franche-Comté. There are many makers of kosher goat's cheese. Check Sources to buy these and other kosher cheeses.

Chestnuts. This sweet edible nut is used in both savoury and sweet dishes – and even as a snack. I recommend whole, peeled and roasted chestnuts – peeling them yourself can be a chore – which come in foil bags. I use Galil brand, an Israeli product.

Chicken Livers. If your butcher doesn't sell kashered chicken livers, which aren't otherwise available commercially, you must kasher them yourself following kosher law. To do so, remove any fat from the livers. Rinse them three times under running water, and salt lightly with kosher salt. Transfer the livers to a rack that, when fitted in a roasting pan, will allow juices to run away from it into the pan. Grill the livers until well done, about 5 minutes per side. Cut open a liver to ensure that no pink remains, and grill longer, if necessary. Rinse the livers three times and dry thoroughly.

Chocolate. There are many brands of kosher chocolate available, both domestic and imported, sweetened and unsweetened. Before buying and cooking with them, read labels to determine whether the chocolate is dairy or pareve. Most dark chocolate is dairy-free. Dark chocolate brands I prefer include Swiss-made Alprose, Scharfen Berger and kosher-certified Callebaut, a wonderful chocolate that isn't, however, always available.

Extracts and Colourings. Kosher extracts, such as vanilla or almond, and food colours are widely available. I use Nielsen-Massey, Silver Spoon or Dr. Oetker for most flavours. Java Juice makes an excellent coffee extract. Look for Sugarflair for most food colourings.

Konnyaku. Made from yam flour, konnyaku (sometimes called konjac) has been produced in Japan for centuries. It's extremely healthful, has almost no calories and comes in various seafood flavours, including prawn. I use it to make dumpling fillings. Don't confuse konnyaku noodles or jelly powder with the seafood-shaped product I recommend, which is also sold as 'vegan prawns'. The brand I use is prawn-flavoured Sophie's Kitchen.

Moulard Duck Breast. Moulard or Barbary ducks are large animals with ample, deeply flavourful breasts. By 'breast' I refer to a magret, or half-breast. Check Sources for good suppliers.

Panko. Japanese breadcrumbs used to coat foods for frying or sautéing. Oblong panko are flakier than their Western counterparts, and thus produce particularly delicate crusts. Kikkoman is my brand of choice.

Praline Paste. Used in baking and sweet making, this smooth paste is made by combining equal quantities of skinned hazelnuts (or hazelnuts and almonds) and liquid caramel. When the caramel hardens, it's ground until creamy. I use Bakers Choice praline paste, which comes in tins but you can also easily make your own.

Ramen Noodles. These fresh and dried Japanese noodles are made from flour, salt and water. It's the dried version I call for, available as Tradition Ramen Noodle Soup, a soup-mix kit that also contains a flavour packet. Use the noodles and save the packet for another use.

Sausage. A great variety of kosher sausage is made from virtually all meats – except, of course, pork. You can find merguez, andouille and bratwurst as well as sweet and hot Italian sausage. For the recipes in this book, I use sweet Italian sausage. Ask your butcher for the house brand.

Smoked Dark Meat Turkey. A fine ham substitute, this is widely available in two forms: legs (or 'drumsticks') and 'shwarma', which is made from the thigh. Either will do for the recipes in this book. If you can't find smoked dark meat turkey, use certified (if necessary) turkey pastrami instead.

Surimi. A seafood stand-in, surimi is a traditional Japanese product. Kosher brands contain fish, various food starches, and seafood flavouring, among other ingredients. Sometimes formed to resemble the shellfish it's mimicking, surimi is best used in dishes like my crab cakes and California rolls. Dyna-Sea, which makes prawn and crab surimi, is my brand of choice.

Tofu. A traditional Chinese and Japanese product, tofu is made from curdled soya milk. It's low in fat and cholesterol, protein-rich and very nutritious. Tofu is available in extra-firm, firm, soft and silken styles. I recommend firm tofu for recipes in this book. I've used various brands of kosher tofu over the years, and all have been top-notch.

Wonton Wrappers. Made from flour, eggs and salt, the wrappers can be used in many ways not – to make kreplach, for example. They're available in packets in a variety of forms – round and square, thick and thin.

Courgette Flowers These deliciously edible flowers come from the summer squash. They're available from late spring to early autumn in specialist greengrocers or at farmers' markets. Buy fresh-looking flowers with closed buds. Because the flowers are extremely perishable, store them in the fridge for no more than a day.

chapter

2

Hors d'Oeuvres
and Starters

Hors d'Oeuvres and Starters

Modern starters begin with today's wonderfully expanded kosher store cupboard. Until kosher coconut milk became available, for example, you'd have had to pay serious kitchen dues to make the addictive – and versatile – peanut sauce accompaniment to Chicken and Beef Satays, a real crowd-pleaser. The availability of artisanal kosher cheeses has also made it possible to enjoy hors d'oeuvres like Roasted Portobello Mushrooms with Goat's Cheese and Asian Vinaigrette as well as any dish requiring real Parmesan.

Today's kosher storecupboard also boasts konnyaku and surimi, two traditional Japanese products that provide alluring seafood-like flavour and texture. I use the former in the filling of my Modern Dumplings, toothy pareve bites that also rely on one of my kitchen staples, kosher wonton wrappers. With these on hand, you can make a wide variety of special hors d'oeuvres, as well as kreplach, without any hassle.

Many cooks know that earthy shiitake mushrooms make a great meat stand-in, but think along with me, and you'll make meatless 'meat' dishes that really excite. For example, I add pine nuts and tofu to the shiitake-based filling for Shiitake-Tofu Dumplings with Ginger-Spring Onion Dipping

Sauce. The nuts give a 'rounding' unctuousness to the filling whose flavour is mellowed by the tofu. There's no butter or milk involved, yet there *seems* to be.

I also like to 'upgrade' fats to produce finer results. We all know about chicken fat as a dairy-fat alternative, but think beyond the box, as I did when creating Sautéd Chicken Livers with Warm Cognac Vinaigrette Over Wilted Greens, and use duck fat, which is free for the taking when you roast a duck, or available from your butcher. I partner my ceviche with avocado not only for flavour but to add non-dairy richness to the sprightly fish, which benefits from the buttery contrast while remaining pareve.

I'm particularly proud of the duck prosciutto in this chapter. Following an easy curing method, duck breast is transformed into 'ham' that rivals the genuine article. I serve duck prosciutto with grilled figs, a traditional pairing, but it's truly a gift that keeps on giving. I use the uncut ends to make lardons or julienne it to garnish soups or salads, and save the fat to use in pasta sauces. You get all the flavour of fine ham but without ham. Modern thinking at its best.

Duck Prosciutto

serves 4

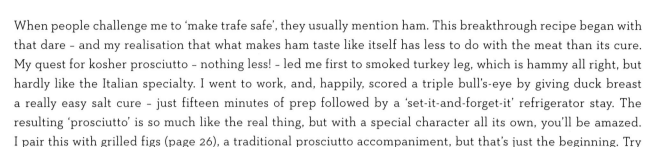

When people challenge me to 'make trafe safe', they usually mention ham. This breakthrough recipe began with that dare – and my realisation that what makes ham taste like itself has less to do with the meat than its cure. My quest for kosher prosciutto – nothing less! – led me first to smoked turkey leg, which is hammy all right, but hardly like the Italian specialty. I went to work, and, happily, scored a triple bull's-eye by giving duck breast a really easy salt cure – just fifteen minutes of prep followed by a 'set-it-and-forget-it' refrigerator stay. The resulting 'prosciutto' is so much like the real thing, but with a special character all its own, you'll be amazed. I pair this with grilled figs (page 26), a traditional prosciutto accompaniment, but that's just the beginning. Try it draped over melon, wrapped around asparagus spears or, diced and sautéed, as a salad garnish.

Geila's Tips

To achieve paper-thin slices, I use an inexpensive electric slicer, a great kitchen investment.

The very ends of the cured breast become over-dried. Save them to put in soup. If you can't find Barbary breasts, place the meat sides of two regular duck breasts together.

2 large Barbary duck breasts (about 300g; see page 19)

510–580g kosher salt

½ teaspoon ground coriander

½ teaspoon ground fennel

½ teaspoon freshly ground black pepper

240ml white wine vinegar

1. Over a burner flame, singe away any remaining pinfeathers from the breasts. Rinse the breasts and dry with kitchen paper.

2. In a deep sided dish just large enough to hold the breasts, make a 2.5cm bed of salt. Place the breasts on the salt and cover with another 2.5cm of salt. Cover with cling film and refrigerate for 24 to 48 hours.

3. In a small bowl, combine the coriander, fennel, and pepper. Holding the breasts over the sink, rinse with the vinegar (to remove the salt), and then under cold running water. Dry the breasts and rub all over with the spice mixture. Wrap the breasts, meat sides together, in two layers of clean muslin. Tie securely with string, making a loop as you do so, and hang the breasts in the fridge. It's important that the air can circulate freely around the meat and the temperature of the fridge does not exceed 4°C/40°F. Leave for about 2 weeks, until the breasts feels firm but not dry. Start checking after a week. Thinner or smaller breasts will take less time.

4. Using an electric slicer or a sharp carving knife, slice the breasts paper-thin or as thinly as possible.

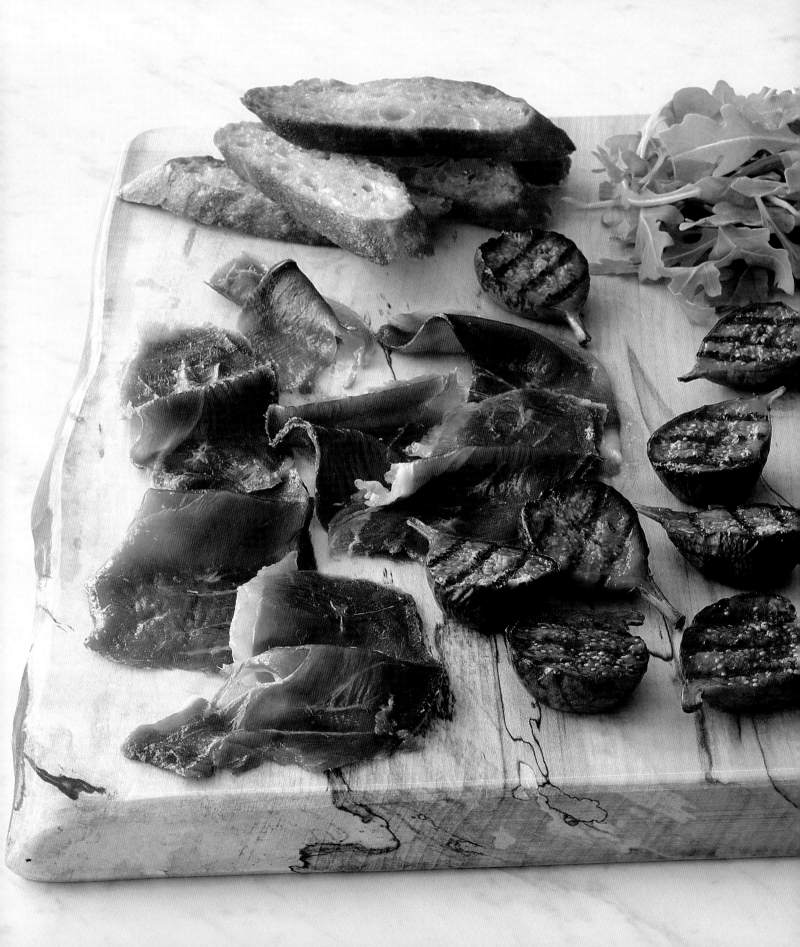

Grilled Figs with Balsamic Gastrique
serves 4

There's nothing as delicious as fresh figs, unless it's grilled figs drizzled with sweet-sour balsamic gastrique. Quickly made yet impressive, these are perfect served with duck prosciutto, over greens dressed with a light vinaigrette, or with goat's cheese. Use the balsamic gastrique as you would fine old balsamic vinegar, drizzled sparingly over savoury dishes. You can also use it as the basis of a sweet and sour sauce.

Geila's Tip

Depending on the degree of ripeness, the figs may need to be cooked a minute more or less than indicated.

Balsamic Gastrique (makes 120ml)
100g sugar
80ml balsamic vinegar

4 tablespoons balsamic gastrique, made with light brown soft sugar
¼ teaspoon cracked black pepper
6 large ripe figs, halved lengthways
2 tablespoons extra-virgin olive oil

1. First make the balsamic gastrique. In a small glass bowl, combine the sugar and vinegar. Microwave at full power for 30 seconds, or until the liquid has boiled and becomes syrupy. Alternatively, combine the ingredients in a small saucepan and bring to a simmer over a medium heat. Reduce the heat and simmer until thickened, about 15 minutes. Leave to cool.

2. Transfer the balsamic gastrique to a medium bowl. Add the pepper and figs, and toss to coat. Marinate for 20 minutes.

3. Meanwhile, preheat a barbecue or the grill, or use a griddle pan. If grilling, cover a baking tray with foil.

4. Brush the barbecue rack, griddle pan or the baking tray with the oil. If using a barbecue or griddle pan, grill the figs skin side up over a medium-high heat until grill marks appear, about 2 minutes. Turn the figs and grill until just beginning to soften, about 1 minute more. If using the grill, grill the figs skin side up until lightly browned, about 1 minute, turn, and cook for 2 minutes. Divide among plates, drizzle with the balsamic gastrique and serve.

Liver Two Ways
Sautéed Chicken Livers with Warm Cognac Vinaigrette Over Wilted Greens

serves 4

I love chopped chicken liver, but sometimes I like to make it into a more elegant starter. This dish, which features the livers served over wilted frisée, combines the best of two worlds, savoury appetiser and salad. The vinaigrette, with its shallot and cognac notes, is particularly enticing. I always follow this with a lighter main course.

1. If using the Duck Prosciutto, heat a small frying pan over a medium heat, and sauté the prosciutto until brown and the fat has rendered, about 4 minutes. Reserve 1 tablespoon of the fat. Remove the duck with a slotted spoon, drain on kitchen paper, and set aside.

2. Increase the heat to medium-high, or if using chicken fat, add 1 tablespoon to a small frying pan over a medium-high heat. When hot, add the shallots, and sauté until browned, about 3 minutes. Add the cognac, and reduce by half, about 2 minutes. Add the mustard, vinegar, sugar and olive oil. Remove the pan from the heat and blend well. Set aside.

3. Spread the flour on a large plate, add the livers, and dredge. In a large frying pan, heat the reserved duck fat, or the remaining tablespoon of chicken fat, with the grapeseed oil over a medium-high heat. Working in batches, if necessary, add the livers and sauté, turning once, until cooked through, about 4 minutes. Set the livers aside.

4. Wipe out the pan with kitchen paper. Return the pan to the heat, add the frisée and half of the vinaigrette, and sauté, tossing, until the frisée has wilted, 35-40 seconds. Divide the frisée among 4 serving plates, top with the livers, sprinkle with the prosciutto, if using, and drizzle the remaining vinaigrette. Serve immediately.

55g Duck Prosciutto (page 24; optional)

2 tablespoons duck fat (see Step 1), or chicken fat

2 shallots, chopped

60ml cognac, sherry or port

2 teaspoons mustard

2 tablespoons balsamic vinegar

2 tablespoons sugar

4 tablespoons extra-virgin olive oil

4 tablespoons flour

450g chicken livers (see pages 18–19 for kashering)

1 tablespoon grapeseed or rapeseed oil

225g frisée, rinsed, dried, torn into bite-sized pieces

Chicken Liver Crostini

makes 12 hors d'oeuvres; serves 4 as a starter

People are sometimes surprised that other cultures have chopped chicken liver. The Italians do a great version that's spread on toasted bread – crostini – and that usually includes capers. My take is enticingly herby and uses breadcrumbs, which give it a wonderful texture. The liver may be served while still warm, cooled or even cold and demands a hearty red wine in accompaniment!

5 tablespoons duck or chicken fat

1 small onion, sliced thin and roughly chopped

1 sprig fresh rosemary

¼ teaspoon chilli flakes

2 garlic cloves, flattened with the side of a knife

½ teaspoon fresh or dried oregano

½ teaspoon fresh or dried sage

2 tablespoons chopped small capers, rinsed and drained

225g chicken livers (see pages 18-19 for kashering)

½ teaspoon kosher salt, plus more

½ teaspoon freshly ground black pepper, plus more

120ml white wine

2 slices white sandwich bread, crusts removed

1 baguette, diagonally sliced into 12 pieces

2 tablespoons extra-virgin olive oil

1. In a large frying pan, heat 2 tablespoons of the fat over a medium-high heat. Add the onion, rosemary, red pepper and garlic, and sauté, stirring, until the onion is translucent, about 5 minutes. Add the oregano, sage and capers, and sauté, stirring, until the onions are beginning to brown, about 5 minutes. Transfer the mixture to a plate and remove and dispose of the rosemary sprigs.

2. Add the remaining fat to the pan and heat over a medium-high heat. Sprinkle the livers with the salt and pepper on both sides and sauté until cooked through, turning once, about 2 minutes. Return the onion mixture to the pan, add the wine, and cook for 2 minutes. Transfer the livers to a plate, and cook the wine until it has reduced to 60ml, 3-4 minutes.

3. Meanwhile, pulse the sandwich bread in a food processor to make rough crumbs. Add the livers and onion mixture and pulse until a rough paste is formed. Season with salt and pepper, and transfer to a medium bowl. Cover and chill, if not serving immediately.

4. Preheat the oven to 170ºC/gas mark 3. Brush the baguette slices on both sides with the oil, transfer to a baking sheet and bake until lightly toasted, about 10 minutes. Spread the liver mixture on the slices and serve.

Chicken and Beef Satays with Peanut Dipping Sauce

makes 24 hors d'oeuvres; serves 6 as a starter

These satays are one of my favourite bites, but it's the peanut sauce that makes this dish so special. It's based on others I've enjoyed over the years, but couldn't make until kosher-certified coconut milk became available. You'll love the way its lime-brightened zing plays against the smoky meat, itself deeply flavoured with garlic, cumin and ginger.

---

1. To make the satays, using a very sharp carving knife, cut the chicken and/or beef into 0.5cm-thick slices, 15cm long by 5cm wide.

2. In a medium bowl, combine the soy sauce, oil, shallots, lime zest, ginger, garlic, turmeric, cumin and coriander. If using only chicken or beef, transfer the mixture to a large sealable freezer bag or suitable container and add the chicken or beef. If using both chicken and beef, divide the marinade between two large sealable freezer bags and add the chicken to one and the beef to the other. Seal the bag(s) and marinate refrigerated for at least 1 hour.

3. Meanwhile, make the peanut sauce. In a large saucepan, combine the coconut milk, peanut butter and chicken stock, and whisk to blend. Cook over a medium heat until the mixture simmers, stirring often to prevent scorching, about 5 minutes. Add the tomato, turmeric, cumin, garlic, curry paste, if using, and sugar, and mix well. Simmer until the flavours have blended, about 15 minutes. Season with salt. If the sauce is too thick, add up to 120ml of water and blend. Cover and refrigerate the sauce for up to 2 days, or keep at room temperature if making the satays immediately. Just before serving, reheat and blend in the lime juice and coriander.

4. Thread the strips concertina-style onto the skewers, one type of meat for each. Preheat the grill, or heat a griddle pan or large heavy frying pan over a high heat. If using a frying pan or griddle pan, spray the interior with non-stick cooking spray; if grilling, line a baking tray with foil and spray. Grill or fry, turning once, until the meat is just cooked through, 4-6 minutes total. Transfer the skewers to a warm platter and serve with the sauce.

Convert It

To make the peanut sauce pareve, substitute vegetable stock (page 195) for the chicken stock. Made this way, it's excellent served with grilled fish.

Satays

900g boneless skinless chicken, light or dark meat, and/or sirloin, chilled in the freezer for 2 hours

60ml soy sauce

60ml rapeseed oil

2 large shallots, finely chopped

1 tablespoon lime zest

1 teaspoon grated ginger

2 garlic cloves, smashed with the flat of a knife

1½ teaspoons turmeric

1 teaspoon cumin

3 tablespoons chopped coriander

24 bamboo skewers, soaked in water for 1 hour

Peanut Sauce

300ml coconut milk

115g smooth peanut butter

120ml chicken stock

3 medium tomatoes, skinned, deseeded and cut into 0.5cm dice

1½ teaspoons turmeric

1 teaspoon cumin

1 tablespoon finely chopped garlic

½ tablespoon harissa, Thai red curry paste or hot sauce (optional)

3 tablespoons light brown soft sugar

kosher salt

2 tablespoons fresh lime juice

3-4 tablespoons chopped coriander, to taste

Roasted Portobello Mushrooms with Goat Cheese and Asian Vinaigrette

serves 6

Everyone loves the special earthiness of roasted mushrooms. My version pairs portobellos with goat's cheese, which is now available in great kosher-certified types, and a sprightly salad. My secret is the Asian Vinaigrette, a real flavour powerhouse that's both hot and just sweet enough. This gets any meal off to the best start.

Convert It

To make this into a pareve dish, omit the cheese.

Geila's Tip

You can plate and refrigerate the greens and mushrooms and prepare the vinaigrette ahead. Bring the salad to room temperature and dress it just before serving.

6 garlic cloves

60ml extra-virgin olive oil

½ teaspoon kosher salt

3 large portobello mushrooms, stemmed, wiped with damp kitchen paper

Vinaigrette

60ml freshly squeezed lemon juice

30ml soy sauce

2 garlic cloves, finely chopped

½ teaspoon kosher salt

2 tablespoons sugar

3 drops hot chilli oil

180ml grapeseed or rapeseed oil

350g mesclun or other mixed salad leaves

140g goat's cheese, crumbled

1. Preheat the oven to 200ºC/gas mark 6. Cover a baking tray with foil.

2. In a small food processor, combine the garlic, olive oil and salt, and process until roughly puréed. Alternatively, chop the garlic and combine in a small bowl with the olive oil and salt, and whisk to blend.

3. Brush both sides of the mushroom caps with the mixture and transfer to the baking tray. Bake the mushrooms until golden and most of their liquid has evaporated, turning once, about 35 minutes. Cool to room temperature and slice 1cm thick. Set aside.

4. To make the vinaigrette, place all of the ingredients except the grapeseed oil in a blender and blend. With the motor still running, drizzle in the grapeseed oil until the mixture has thickened. Alternatively, place the ingredients in a large measuring jug and use a hand blender. Adjust the seasoning.

5. Place the greens in a large bowl, drizzle with 80ml of the vinaigrette, and toss until the leaves are evenly coated. If the salad seems dry, add more vinaigrette and toss again.

6. Divide the greens among 6 serving plates. Surround one side with portobello slices and add crumbles of goat's cheese on the other side. Serve.

Courgette Flowers with Two Fillings:
Sun-Dried Tomatoes, Basil and Cheese
Polenta, Sweetcorn and Crème Fraîche
serves 6

At a picking farm one summer I was delighted to discover squash flowers free for the taking. I've always loved them stuffed, and once home, set about devising my own fillings. Anything stuffed with cheese then fried is irresistible – thus my ricotta and Parmesan filling, made lively with sun-dried tomatoes. The polenta stuffing is a maize double-whammy – it's got sweetcorn kernels as well as the polenta – plus crème fraîche for richness. Stuffed either way (or both), these make a terrific starter or hot hors d'oeuvre that's also fun to do.

Geila's Tips

Out of season, find courgette flowers in specialist greengrocers.

The coating is a tempura-batter variation that produces a thin, crunchy bite. Make sure to chill it, as directed.

25g cornflour

12 courgette flowers (see Tip), pistils removed, any attached courgette retained (see Step 2)

Tomato, Basil and Cheese Filling

227g ricotta

1 medium egg

16–17g grated Parmesan

25g sun-dried tomatoes in oil, drained, cut into 0.5cm dice

1 small garlic clove, finely chopped

1 tablespoon chopped fresh basil

pinch nutmeg

pinch kosher salt

Batter

45g plain flour

80g rice flour

240ml carbonated water

480ml grapeseed or rapeseed oil, for frying

sea salt or kosher salt

1. Line a baking tray with baking paper and dust with the cornflour.

2. Using damp kitchen paper, very gently clean the flowers, if necessary. (If a small courgette is attached to a flower, without removing it, slice it lengthways into thirds.)

3. In a small bowl, combine the filling ingredients and blend. Handling the flowers very gently, spoon or pipe 1½ to 2 tablespoons of the filling into them, twisting the flowers to close them. Transfer the flowers to the baking tray and refrigerate until ready to fry.

4. Preheat the oven to 80ºC. Fill a large bowl half full with ice water. In a second bowl that fits in the first, combine the flours for the batter. Whisk in the carbonated water just to blend; the batter doesn't have to be completely smooth. Place the second bowl in the first and refrigerate both until the batter is very cold, 15–30 minutes.

5. Heat the oil in a deep frying pan over a high heat until 190ºC. Working in batches of two, dip the flowers (and the courgette, if attached) into the batter, shake off any excess and fry until golden and crisp, 2–3 minutes. Using a slotted spoon, transfer the flowers to the baking tray. Place the tray in the oven with the door slightly ajar to keep them warm. Repeat with the remaining flowers.

6. Transfer 2 flowers to small warmed serving plates. Sprinkle with the salt and serve.

Polenta, Sweetcorn and Crème Fraîche Filling

I use shop-bought, prepared polenta for this, but you can make your own, if you like.

1. Bring a medium pot of water to the boil. Add the cobs and cook until just tender, about 2 minutes. Drain, cool the corn, and cut off the kernels. Transfer to a medium bowl and set aside.

2. Heat the butter and oil in a medium sauté pan over a medium heat. Add the onion and jalapeño and sauté, stirring, until the onion is translucent and the pepper soft, about 10 minutes. Transfer to the corn bowl, add the polenta and crème fraîche, and season with the salt and pepper. Blend well, stuff the flowers with the filling and fry as directed above.

2 corn on the cobs, or 140g frozen and defrosted sweetcorn

1 tablespoon unsalted butter

1 tablespoon rapeseed oil

1 small onion, chopped

1 jalapeño pepper, deseeded, finely chopped

150g prepared polenta, soft

110g crème fraîche

kosher salt and freshly ground black pepper

Ceviche with Avocado and Tortilla Chips

serves 6

Here's a confession: I never serve gefilte fish. That favourite has been replaced on my table by this more exciting dish, which will do wonders for your menu as a starter or light main. Tangy with fresh lime, the ceviche also pairs buttery avocado and crunchy chips, a terrific textural play. And the dish almost makes itself, a big plus when you've got other cooking to do.

Geila's Tips

To dismantle an avocado for slicing, first cut it lengthways and gently twist the halves apart. Embed the stone on the blade-heel of a large knife, twist and lift to remove the stone. Peel the avocado, then slice the flesh as required.

I've found that jalapeños with a brown line or veins on the outside are hotter than those without.

680g summer flounder or other non-oily, white-fleshed fish, cut into bite-sized pieces (about 2.5cm square)

1 medium tomato, skinned, deseeded and cut into 0.5cm dice

4 spring onions, white parts only, finely sliced

20g chopped coriander

½ mango, cut into 0.5cm dice (optional)

2 garlic cloves, finely chopped

½ jalapeño, deseeded and finely chopped

80ml fruity, extra-virgin olive oil

80ml freshly squeezed lime juice

½ teaspoon kosher salt, or to taste

2 avocados, sliced 0.5cm thick

tortilla chips, for serving

1. In a medium non-porous bowl, combine the fish, tomato, spring onions, coriander and mango, if using.

2. In a separate small bowl or large measuring jug, combine the garlic, jalapeño, oil, lime juice and salt, and stir to blend. Pour the mixture over the fish and toss gently. Cover and refrigerate for at least 3 hours.

3. Strain the ceviche. Using a slotted spoon, fill a 115g ramekin with the ceviche. Tip to drain any excess liquid and unmould it onto the centre of each serving plate. Alternatively, mound portions of the ceviche onto the plates. Fan the avocado around the ceviche, garnish with the chips, and serve.

Mango Salad with Sherry-Shallot Vinaigrette

serves 6

I never tire of this salad. What makes it so special is its play of sweet and tart – of delectable mango with sherry vinegar and shallot bite. Rocket, endive and toasted pine nuts add more flavour layers. Mango is now available all year round. For this recipe, I always choose slightly under-ripe fruit, which is tarter than more mature kinds, but either will do. You can gild the lily by garnishing the salad with crumbled feta or blue cheese, but it's great as is.

Geila's Tip

You may not need all the dressing the recipe makes, but any extra is money in the fridge. Use it for salads made with peaches or other fruit, or tart or bitter greens, such as endive or chicory.

120ml plus 1 teaspoon rapeseed oil

65g pine nuts

2 large shallots, roughly chopped

60ml sherry vinegar

2 tablespoons fresh lemon juice

½ teaspoon kosher salt or more, if needed

2 tablespoons honey

60ml extra-virgin olive oil

6 large handfuls of baby rocket

2 medium heads chicory, sliced into 2.5cm pieces

65–80g red onion, finely sliced

1 large mango, cut into 2.5cm dice

1. In a small frying pan, heat the 1 teaspoon of oil over a medium-low heat. Add the pine nuts and toast them, tossing frequently, until lightly coloured and fragrant, about 3 minutes. Set aside.

2. In a large measuring jug, combine the shallots, vinegar, lemon juice, salt, honey, olive oil and remaining rapeseed oil. Using a hand or stand blender, blend well. Adjust the seasoning, if necessary.

3. In a large serving bowl, combine the rocket, endive, onions, mango and the pine nuts. Drizzle over half of the dressing and toss. Add more dressing if the salad seems dry. Adjust the seasoning, toss again, and serve.

Dumplings Two Ways
Revolution Dumplings with Orange-Ginger Dipping Sauce
makes 48

Sometimes fate hands you just what you're looking for. A while ago I was planning an Asian-themed cocktail party and dared myself to make pareve 'prawn'-filled dumplings. My challenge took me to Chinatown in Manhattan, where I discovered (in a vegan grocery shop!) konnyaku, a traditional Japanese product made from yam flour. It comes in various flavours including prawn.

These delicious dumplings can be steamed, fried or simmered, and all three options are given below, but the last must be done watchfully as the wrappers can break if the water boils. No need to worry about elaborate wrapper pleating; the basic triangular kreplach fold works beautifully.

1. Using a food processor, pulse the konnyaku until it's finely chopped. Transfer to a medium bowl and combine with the remaining dumpling ingredients except the wonton skins. Stir to blend.

2. To form the dumplings, place about 1 teaspoon of the filling in the centre of each wrapper. Moisten two edges of the wrapper with water, fold to make a triangle, and press the edges to seal in the filling.

3. Preheat the oven to 90°C and put a pan of hot water in it, for moisture. To steam the dumplings, use either a bamboo steamer or a roasting pan with a fitted rack. In a saucepan, if using the steamer, or in the roasting pan, bring 0.5cm–1cm of water to a simmer over a medium heat. Line the steamer with cabbage leaves and lightly spray with non-stick vegetable cooking spray, or lightly spray the steamer's surface or rack. Place as many dumplings as will fit into the steamer, or onto the rack, without touching each other. Cover and steam until the edges of the wrappers appear soft, 3–5 minutes. Transfer the dumplings from the steamer or rack to a heatproof platter and place in the oven to keep warm. Repeat until all the dumplings are cooked.

To fry the dumplings, heat a large non-stick frying pan on a medium-high heat. Add 1 tablespoon of vegetable oil and when hot, add as many dumplings as will comfortably fit. Sauté, turning once, until lightly brown, about 1 minute per side. Repeat until all the dumplings are cooked. To simmer the dumplings, fill a roasting pan three-quarters full with water. Bring the water to the boil, reduce the heat to barely simmering, and slide in as many dumplings as will comfortably fit. Simmer until the wrapper edges appear soft, about 5 minutes. Remove with a perforated spoon and repeat until all the dumplings are cooked. Keep warm as directed above.

4. Meanwhile, to make the dipping sauce, combine the soy sauce, ginger and orange juice with 2 tablespoons of water.

5. Transfer the dumplings to serving plates and serve with the sauce.

Geila's Tips

Uncooked dumplings freeze very well. Place them onto a baking tray, sprinkle with cornflour (to prevent sticking), freeze, then transfer to a freezer bag for long-term storage.

If you have difficulty finding konnyaku, you can use surimi, a fish-based product that has a distinct prawn flavour.

Dumplings

1 x 170g or 225g packet of prawn-style konnyaku or prawn-stick surimi

40–50g diced water chestnuts

17g finely sliced spring onions, white parts and a bit of green

10g chopped coriander

1 egg white

1 tablespoon soy sauce

1 tablespoon mirin

1 tablespoon toasted sesame oil

¼ teaspoon chilli oil

48 wonton wrappers

Dipping Sauce

120ml soy sauce

1½ teaspoons grated ginger

2 tablespoons orange juice

Shiitake-Tofu Dumplings with Ginger–Spring Onion Dipping Sauce

makes 48

I devised these delicious dumplings to pair with my konnyaku-based version, whose filling tastes like prawn. I wanted something pareve that also tasted meaty. I thought of shiitake mushrooms, which have a meaty savour – too much so, it turned out. So I added tofu, which tamed the shiitakes perfectly. I also included Chinese cabbage for crunch. Served with a sprightly ginger-based dipping sauce, these make a perfect nibble.

Geila's Tip

These can also be fried – see Step 3, page 41.

85g dried shiitakes

100g pine nuts

115g firm tofu, drained on kitchen paper

250g Chinese cabbage, finely sliced, plus leaves, for lining a steamer

4 garlic cloves, roasted

2 tablespoons soy sauce

1 teaspoon grated or finely chopped ginger

1 tablespoon mirin

2 tablespoons rice vinegar

kosher salt

½ teaspoon hot chilli oil (optional)

1 egg white, if needed

48 wonton wrappers

Dipping Sauce

3 tablespoons soy sauce

1 spring onion, white part only, finely chopped

1 teaspoon grated ginger

3 drops hot chilli oil

1 tablespoon sugar

1. Place the mushrooms in a small bowl and add hot water to cover. Soak until the mushrooms are soft, about 30 minutes.

2. Drain the mushrooms (strain and reserve the soaking liquid for soup or stock) and transfer to a food processor. Add the nuts, tofu, cabbage and garlic. Pulse until finely chopped, and transfer to a medium bowl. Add the soy sauce, ginger, mirin and vinegar. Season with the salt, add the chilli oil, if using, and blend. If the mixture seems crumbly, add the egg white and mix well.

3. Place the wonton wrappers on a work surface. Place 1 teaspoon of the filling in the centre of the wrappers. Moisten two adjacent edges with water, and fold to make a triangle. Seal the dumplings by pressing the edges. Repeat with the remaining wrappers.

4. Preheat the oven on a very low setting (90°C) and put a pan of hot water in it, for moisture. To steam the dumplings, use either a bamboo steamer or a roasting pan with a fitted rack. In a pot, if using the steamer, or in the roasting pan, bring 0.5–1cm of water to a simmer over a medium heat. Line the steamer with cabbage leaves and lightly spray with non-stick vegetable cooking spray, or lightly spray the steamer's surface or rack. Place as many dumplings as will fit into the steamer, or on the rack, without touching each other. Cover and steam until the edges of the wrappers appear soft, 3–5 minutes. Transfer the dumplings to a heatproof platter and place in the oven to keep warm. Repeat until all the dumplings are cooked.

5. Meanwhile, to make the dipping sauce, in a small bowl, combine all the ingredients plus 2 tablespoons of water and stir.

6. Transfer the dumplings to plates and serve with the sauce.

Fried Pea and Parmesan Ravioli

makes 24 hors d'oeuvres; serves 6 as a starter

You probably don't think of peas and Parmesan as a culinary combo, but they're fabulous together. These quick-to-do fried ravioli feature a filling made from that coupling plus ricotta for creaminess and a bit of mint, a real pea flavour enhancer. The wonton wrappers fry beautifully – my hors d'oeuvre store cupboard would be bare without them. These make a great starter too.

1. Put the peas in a colander and place under hot running water to defrost them. Drain and set aside.

2. In a small frying pan, heat the 1 teaspoon of oil over a medium-low heat. Add the pine nuts and toast them, tossing frequently, until lightly coloured and fragrant, about 3 minutes. Transfer the nuts to a food processor.

3. Add the peas, ricotta, Parmesan, garlic, salt, nutmeg and mint to the processor, and pulse until a paste is formed. Adjust the seasoning, if necessary.

5. Line a baking sheet with baking paper. Place 4 wrappers on a dry work surface. Place 1 tablespoon of the filling in the centre of each, brush two adjacent edges with a little water (or use your fingertip), fold on the diagonal, and pinch to seal. Repeat with the remaining filling and wrappers. If not frying immediately, refrigerate or freeze the ravioli.

6. Fill a large heavy frying pan with 1cm of oil and heat over a medium heat until the oil is 175ºC. Alternatively, test the heat of the oil by placing a corner of a ravioli in it; the oil is ready if the corner sizzles. Working in batches, fry the ravioli without crowding until lightly golden (see Tip), turning once with a slotted spoon, about 2 minutes. Transfer the ravioli to kitchen paper and sprinkle with salt. Transfer to a serving dish and serve.

Geila's Tip

Remove the ravioli from the oil while they're one shade lighter than you want them to be. They'll continue to colour after cooking.

225g frozen peas

1 teaspoon grapeseed or rapeseed oil, plus more for frying

32g pine nuts

227g ricotta, drained using a colander or sieve

17g grated Parmesan

1 garlic clove

½ teaspoon kosher salt, plus more for sprinkling

⅛ teaspoon nutmeg

2 tablespoons chopped mint

24 wonton wrappers

chapter

3

Soups

Soups

Soups are at the heart of kosher cooking – think golden chicken soup. Until now, though, many soups that use cream for richness or pork for heartiness, not to mention uncertified ingredients, were beyond the kosher cook's reach. With the 'modern' approach, however, the world of soups can be made for kosher enjoyment – and their recipes converted for meat, dairy and pareve.

Take Velvet Chestnut Soup, a lusciously elegant starter. With the advent of kosher-certified roasted chestnuts and truffle oil, this terrific 'meat' dish is not only doable, but can be made dairy or pareve without compromise. Kosher coconut milk, another newcomer to the kosher store cupboard, enriches Coconut–Ginger Squash Soup, an Asian-themed pareve dish than can also be 'meat'. Lentil Soup with 'Ham' gets its hearty, ham-like smokiness from smoked turkey drumstick and, using Parmesan rind, can be a dairy dish too. The rind also flavours Fresh Vegetable Minestrone, where it elevates a dish that, before kosher Parmesan was available, often lacked character.

But 'modern' soups aren't about 'new' flavours only. A creamy soup that's also pareve needs to have the same texture as one made with dairy products or starches. Four-Mushroom Onion Soup with Truffle Oil-Thyme Croûtes uses oil to provide body as does the pareve variation of Creamy Artichoke Soup,

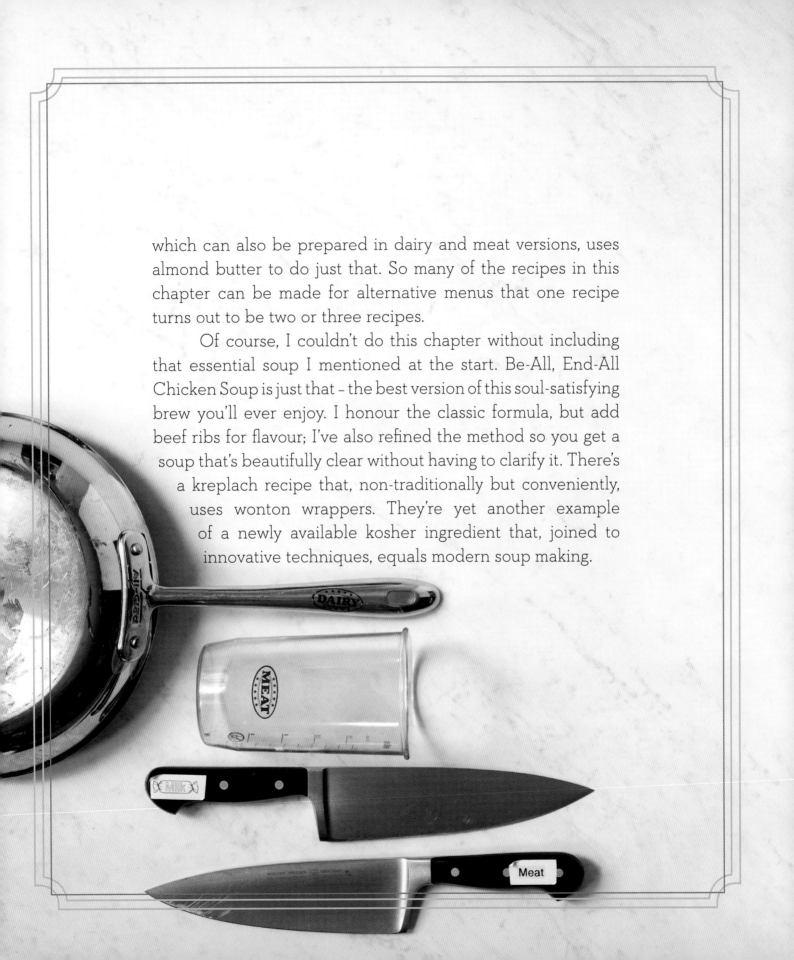

which can also be prepared in dairy and meat versions, uses almond butter to do just that. So many of the recipes in this chapter can be made for alternative menus that one recipe turns out to be two or three recipes.

Of course, I couldn't do this chapter without including that essential soup I mentioned at the start. Be-All, End-All Chicken Soup is just that – the best version of this soul-satisfying brew you'll ever enjoy. I honour the classic formula, but add beef ribs for flavour; I've also refined the method so you get a soup that's beautifully clear without having to clarify it. There's a kreplach recipe that, non-traditionally but conveniently, uses wonton wrappers. They're yet another example of a newly available kosher ingredient that, joined to innovative techniques, equals modern soup making.

Roasted Aubergine and Pepper Soup with Fricos

serves 10–12

I love this delectable soup, which is full of the deep flavours of roasted aubergine and sweet peppers. It's also a great example of three-way cooking – a single dish you can easily modify to make something that works for various menus. The option to thicken the soup with oil rather than with butter or a butter-based roux is key to its versatility. I offer this with fricos – quickly prepared cheese wafers – but you could garnish it with grated Parmesan and fresh ricotta instead.

Convert It

To make this into a meat dish, substitute chicken stock for the vegetable stock and drizzle each serving with Balsamic Gastrique (page 26). For a pareve version, substitute extra-virgin olive oil for the butter, and finish with drops of balsamic vinegar, Balsamic Gastrique or basil leaves.

Geila's Tip

You can make the fricos ahead of time and store them in an airtight container. They're also delicious served with drinks.

5 large aubergines

6 medium red, yellow or orange peppers

2 tablespoons butter

3 tablespoons grapeseed or rapeseed oil

2 large onions, coarsely chopped

4 to 6 large garlic cloves, to taste, finely chopped

50g tomato purée

2.8 litres vegetable stock

salt and freshly ground black pepper

3 or 4 fresh basil leaves

Fricos

75-80g grated Parmesan, Cheddar, Swiss or other hard cheese

1½ to 2 tablespoons plain flour

¼ teaspoon cayenne pepper, or to taste

1. Preheat the oven to 220°C/gas mark 7. Line 1 or 2 medium baking trays, depending on aubergine size, with foil and spray lightly with non-stick cooking spray or grease lightly with vegetable oil.

2. Remove any stems from the aubergines and halve them lengthways. With a fork, prick the skin side of the aubergines all over. Sprinkle the cut sides with salt, place the aubergines skin side up on the tray, and bake until wrinkled and soft, about 40 minutes. Leave to cool, then remove the skin and seeds with your fingers. (If you have difficulty, work the skin off under cold running water.) Chop the aubergines into large chunks.

3. On the hob or under the grill, roast the peppers until the skin is uniformly charred. Transfer to a paper bag or a bowl. Close the bag or cover the bowl with foil, a tea towel or cling film. Allow the peppers to steam until they become cool enough to handle. Remove the stems, peel and seeds, and cut the peppers into 2.5-4cm dice. Reserve any juice.

4. In a heavy saucepan, heat the butter and oil over a medium heat. Add the onion and sauté until translucent, 5-10 minutes. Add the garlic and sauté for 1-2 minutes more. Stir in the peppers, aubergines, tomato purée and stock. Bring to the boil, reduce the heat, and simmer for 1 hour.

5. Using a hand blender (or carefully transferring to a stand blender or food processor in batches), purée the soup. If too thick, add more stock.

6. To make the fricos, combine the ingredients in a small bowl and mix lightly until blended. Transfer to a colander and shake to remove excess flour and any small bits of cheese.

7. Heat a medium non-stick frying pan or a griddle over a medium heat. Add a small handful of the frico mixture and flatten to make a 8cm round. When the cheese has melted and the edges of the frico are slightly coloured, turn carefully with a spatula and cook until coloured. Remove and drape the frico, coloured side up, over a rolling pin. Leave to cool and firm. Repeat with the remaining mixture.

8. Season the soup with salt and pepper, transfer to serving bowls and garnish with the basil. Serve with the fricos.

Lentil Soup with 'Ham'

serves 8-10

In my pre-kosher days I always loved lentil soup with ham or bacon added. Now we have smoked turkey leg, a marvellous kosher alternative to those items and one that tastes absolutely right in this soup. Deeply hearty, this is one of those dishes for which cold weather was invented. Add some bread and a salad and you've got yourself a *meal*.

1. In a heavy-based saucepan, combine the oils and heat over a medium-high heat. Add the onion, celery, garlic and carrots, and sauté, stirring, until softened but without colouring, about 8 minutes. Add the turkey and sauté, stirring, until it begins to crisp and colour, 3-5 minutes. Add the lentils and sauté, stirring, for 2 minutes.

2. Add the stock, bring to the boil, cover, reduce the heat and simmer until the lentils are soft, about 1 hour. Season with the salt and serve.

Convert It

To make this a dairy dish, substitute butter for the olive oil, replace the meat stock with vegetable stock, and add Parmesan rind, or that of another hard, flavourful cheese, in place of the turkey.

1½ tablepoons extra-virgin olive oil

1½ tablespoons grapeseed or rapeseed oil

115g chopped onion

2 celery sticks, chopped

2 garlic cloves, finely chopped

2 medium carrots, peeled and chopped

115g smoked turkey leg, cut into 0.5cm dice

350g green lentils, rinsed

1.9 litres chicken stock

kosher salt

Creamy Artichoke Soup

serves 6

I've always enjoyed artichoke soup, but found it a hassle to make. Dismantling fresh artichokes was a trial - and tinned or marinated hearts wouldn't do at all. Now we have tinned artichoke hearts in water, which give this quickly made soup its deep artichoke flavour. Another special ingredient - almond butter - provides silky creaminess. For a special touch, garnish the soup with julienned Duck Prosciutto (see page 24).

Convert It

To make this a dairy dish, substitute butter for the olive oil, vegetable stock (page 193) for the chicken stock, and 3 tablespoons of grated Parmesan. Add the Parmesan to the soup before puréeing it. To make this pareve, use vegetable stock in place of the chicken stock.

Geila's Tip

Sieving the soup after it's been blended adds a step, but really elevates the dish.

1½ tablespoons extra-virgin olive oil

1½ tablespoons grapeseed or rapeseed oil

60g onion, finely chopped

1 celery stick, finely chopped

1 medium parsnip, peeled, finely chopped

1 garlic clove

340g artichoke hearts

950ml chicken stock

2 tablespoons almond butter

¼ teaspoon freshly ground black pepper

kosher salt

1. In a heavy-based saucepan, combine the oils and heat over a medium-high heat. Add the onion, celery, parsnip and garlic, and sauté, stirring, until the vegetables begin to soften, 8-10 minutes. Add the artichoke hearts and sauté, stirring, until they begin to wilt, about 3 minutes. Add the stock, bring to the boil, reduce the heat and simmer, covered, until the flavours are blended, about 40 minutes.

2. Using a hand blender (or carefully transferring the soup to a stand blender or food processor in batches), purée the soup. Add the almond butter and stir to blend. Add the pepper, season with the salt, and serve.

Velvet Chestnut Soup

serves 10

This super-smooth, sherry-scented soup is a major 'wow', fit for your fanciest entertaining. A touch of honey adds just the right amount of sweetness, and truffle oil – added to the soup and used as a garnish – kicks the dish into the stratosphere. And it's easy to do. The recipe makes a large quantity of soup, but it freezes beautifully. Follow this soup with roasted meat or poultry.

1. In a large stockpot, combine the margarine and oil, and heat over a medium heat. Add the garlic, shallots, leeks and celery, and sauté, stirring, until the vegetables soften without colouring, 10–12 minutes.

2. Add the chestnuts, 3 sprigs of thyme and the bay leaf, and sauté, stirring, until the chestnuts begin to brown, about 20 minutes. Add the white wine, bring to the boil, and cook until evaporated, 10–15 minutes. Add the sherry and 120ml of water, bring to the boil and reduce the liquid by three-quarters, 5–10 minutes. Add the stock, reduce the heat and simmer until the chestnuts fall apart, about 1¹/2 hours.

3. Strain the herbs from the soup, and using a hand blender (or carefully transferring the soup to a stand blender or food processor in batches), purée. Pass the soup through a fine-mesh sieve, working it with a wooden spoon, into a second pan. Season with the salt and pepper, and add the honey. Blend again.

4. With the motor running, add the truffle oil in a thin stream and blend. Adjust the seasoning, if necessary, and transfer to serving bowls. Drizzle with truffle oil, garnish with the thyme sprigs, and serve.

Convert it

To make this a dairy dish, substitute butter for the margarine. To make it pareve, substitute vegetable stock (page 193) for the chicken stock.

Geila's Tip

The recipe directs that the soup be strained before finishing. You can skip this step, but the straining assures a silky texture that sets the soup apart. You'll get a thinner soup, but one with a 'thicker' flavour.

4 tablespoons margarine

60ml grapeseed or rapeseed oil

4 garlic cloves

4 medium shallots, finely sliced

3 leeks, white parts only, well washed and finely sliced

3 celery sticks, cut into 0.5cm dice

1.82kg fresh chestnuts, roasted, peeled and roughly chopped

3 sprigs fresh thyme, plus more for garnishing

1 bay leaf

360ml dry white wine

120ml dry sherry

2.8 litres chicken stock

kosher salt and freshly ground black pepper

4 tablespoons honey

4 tablespoons truffle oil, plus more for garnishing

Be-All, End-All Chicken Soup

serves 12

When a friend asked me for my chicken soup recipe for a party she was giving, I was dumbfounded. I didn't have one! I'd always potchkeyed, producing soup that people said was great. But a recipe was needed, and being me, it had to be the best. After days of trying every soup-making technique known to Jewish womanhood, and producing bathtubs of soup, I arrived at this one - yes, the best. It's everything you want chicken soup to be - rich, hearty, golden and beautifully clear without having to be clarified.

There's no salt in this recipe, so season it to your taste. The onion skin adds colour, but peel the onion if you want a lighter-coloured soup. Save the cooked ribs - it adds rich flavour - for making Kreplach (page 57), which you serve with the soup. Or serve this with vegetables, freshly steamed or from the pot. And enjoy!

Geila's Tip

To clean the leeks, trim the root end. With the tip of a knife, slice the leek from both ends leaving an uncut centre portion about 2.5cm wide. Run the leeks under cold water, separating the layers to remove any grit.

---

4 medium parsnips, peeled and cut into 1cm dice

4 medium celery sticks, cut into thirds

3 leeks, white parts only, well cleaned (see Tip)

1 medium onion, unpeeled, quartered

2 bouquets garnis (2 crushed garlic cloves, 1 bay leaf, ½ bunch dill, ½ bunch flat-leaf parsley, and 4 peppercorns divided among two squares of muslin, knotted to enclose)

450g beef ribs

1 x 1.8–2kg stewing chicken, cut into eight parts, rinsed, any excess fat removed

1.3kg chicken legs, wings and bones, any combination, rinsed, any excess fat removed

1. In a large stockpot, combine the parsnips, celery, leeks, onion and bouquets garnis. Place the ribs on top and then the chicken. Add cold water to cover by 2.5cm. Bring to the boil slowly over a medium heat, 45-60 minutes. Reduce the heat and simmer for 1 hour, skimming to remove any surface solids every 10 minutes. Simmer for another hour, skimming every 20 minutes, and transfer the breast to a medium bowl. Simmer, skimming as needed, for 1¼ hours more. With tongs or a slotted spatula, carefully remove the remaining chicken and the ribs, and transfer to the bowl. (Reserve the chicken, skinned and boned, for chicken salad, or return to the soup. Use the ribs to make kreplach, page 57.)

2. Meanwhile, fill the sink with cold water and add ice. Place a large clean bowl in the sink. Line a colander or sieve that fits over the bowl with a double layer of muslin. Carefully ladle the soup through the muslin, trying not to disturb the ingredients at the bottom of the stockpot. When only a little soup remains, carefully tilt the pot to pour it off. (Discard the pot ingredients.)

3. Allow the soup to cool to room temperature and transfer to the fridge to chill. Remove any solidified fat from the soup and serve, or freeze in a tightly sealed plastic container.

Onion-Stuffed Knaidlach

makes 12; serves 4-6

Growing up, knaidlach – matzo balls – came in one 'flavour' only: hard enough to bounce. Do I hear an amen? I determined to do better, especially after I enjoyed light, parsley-flecked knaidlach at a friend's house. I had a moment of sudden revelation after eating soup-filled buns (*Xiao long bao*) in Chinatown one day – why not stuffed knaidlach? This easy onion-filled version really elevates the traditional matzo ball to great heights, and should become as traditional in your house as it is in mine.

Convert It

To make this a pareve dish, substitute vegetable stock (page 193) for the chicken stock, and rapeseed oil for the chicken fat.

Geila's Tips

You can make the knaidlach ahead and hold them in enough hot soup to cover, or freeze them in a batch of soup. Alternatively, freeze them on a baking tray, then transfer them to sealable bags for freezer storage.

You can either use chicken stock to make these or seltzer, for lightness.

3 medium eggs

5 tablespoons chicken stock or seltzer (see Tips)

5 tablespoons chicken fat or rapeseed oil

¾ teaspoon salt

¼ teaspoon white pepper

6–7g chopped parsley

90g matzo meal

1 large onion, cut into 0.5cm dice

2 tablespoons chopped coriander (optional)

1. In a small bowl, combine the eggs, stock, 3 tablespoons of the fat, salt, pepper and parsley. Add the matzo meal and blend. Cover and refrigerate at least 3 hours or overnight.

2. In a medium frying pan, warm the remaining fat over a medium-high heat. Add the onions and coriander, if using, and sauté, stirring, until translucent and beginning to brown, about 12 minutes. Drain the onions on kitchen paper and set aside.

3. Bring a large saucepan of salted water to the boil. Reduce the heat so the water boils slowly. (Too rapid a boil can make the knaidlach break when cooking.) Using wet hands, form 1–1½ tablespoons each of the matzo meal mixture into a disc held in one palm. Place 1–1½ teaspoons of the onion in the middle of the disc, pinch to enclose, and roll between both hands until a ball is formed. Drop into the water. Repeat with the remaining mixture and onions.

4. When the knaidlach float to the surface of the water, reduce the heat, cover and simmer until tender, 45–60 minutes. Remove the knaidlach with a slotted spoon, transfer to the soup and serve.

Kreplach, Boiled or Fried

makes about 50

One of my favourite memories is making kreplach with my grandma. Their filling was based on regular ground meat. Much later, a girlfriend suggested that I use chopped beef rib instead – a brilliant idea, as the meat is super-tasty. Like Bubbie, I'd always made the wrappers from scratch, but when I was pregnant I just couldn't stand on my feet long enough to do the deed. That's when I discovered versatile wonton wrappers, and I've never looked back. Fried, these make an excellent hors d'oeuvre.

1. Fill a large saucepan with cold water. Add the ribs, and bring to the boil slowly. Skim any solids from the surface. Add the carrots, celery and peppercorns, reduce the heat and simmer until the beef is soft, about 2 hours. (Alternatively, cook the ribs in soup or stock.)

2. Meanwhile, warm the oil in a medium sauté pan over a medium heat. Add the onions, sprinkle with a bit of salt (to help the onions release their liquid) and sauté, stirring, until the onions are golden, 8–10 minutes.

3. When the beef is soft, trim the meat from the bone and cube it. Transfer to a food processor. Add the parsley and pulse until the meat is finely chopped. Transfer the mixture to a medium bowl, add the onions, and season with the salt and pepper. Add one egg and blend; if the mixture seems too thick, add the second egg.

4. To make the kreplach, dust a large sheet of greaseproof paper with the cornflour. Place 4 wrappers on your work surface. Place a teaspoon of the filling in the centre of each wrapper, wet 2 adjacent sides of the wrappers, and fold to form triangles. Press the edges firmly to seal then transfer the kreplach to the greaseproof paper. Repeat with the remaining wrappers.

5. If cooking in liquid, bring a large quantity of salted water to the boil. Add the kreplach and simmer until the wrappers become translucent and soft, 4–5 minutes. Don't allow the kreplach to boil or the skins will break. To fry, fill a medium sauté pan with 2.5cm of vegetable oil, and heat over a medium heat. Working in batches, fry the kreplach, turning once with a slotted skimmer, until they begin to colour, about 2 minutes. Transfer to kitchen paper to drain, season with salt and serve with the Be-All, End-All Chicken Soup on page 54.

Geila's Tips

You can use the cooked beef rib from the Be-All, End-All Chicken Soup on page 54 for the filling. If you do, start making this recipe at Step 3.

The uncooked kreplach freeze beautifully. Put them into barely simmering liquid, or fry them, directly from the freezer.

Extra hands in the kitchen help get the kreplach formed quickly. Here's a case in which I believe in child labour.

1.3kg meaty beef ribs

2 medium carrots, halved

2 celery sticks, halved

4 black peppercorns

3 tablespoons grapeseed or rapeseed oil

3 large onions (about 900g), cut into 0.5cm dice

kosher salt and freshly ground black pepper

20g chopped flat-leaf parsley

1–2 medium eggs, as needed

cornflour, for dusting

50 wonton wrappers

Newly Minted Pea Soup

serves 6

This is the easiest, fastest-to-make elegant soup *ever*. Start to finish, it takes about half an hour – a little more time if you strain it, which gives it a deluxe texture. But it's equally good unstrained, with some chew to it. Tasting exactly like fresh peas, and with just enough mint to highlight their flavour, this is good hot, warm or cold, for fancy meals or everyday dining.

Convert It

To make this a meat dish, substitute olive oil for the butter, and chicken stock for the vegetable stock. Omit the crème fraîche, yogurt or ricotta.

Geila's Tip

Julienned Duck Prosciutto (page 24) makes a great garnish for this.

2 tablespoons butter

2 tablespoons grapeseed or rapeseed oil

2 leeks, white part only, well cleaned (see Tip, page 54), chopped

60g onion, cut into 0.5cm dice

2 garlic cloves, finely chopped

500g frozen peas, defrosted under hot running water

700ml vegetable stock (page 193)

12–15g chopped mint, plus leaves, for garnish

110g crème fraîche, Greek yogurt or ricotta

1. In a medium saucepan over a medium-high, heat the butter and oil. When the foaming subsides, add the leeks, onion and garlic, reduce the heat to medium, and sweat the vegetables until just transparent, about 8 minutes. Add the peas, stir, and cook for 2 minutes. Add the stock and the chopped mint, and simmer for 12 minutes. Add the cream, then using a hand blender (or carefully transferring the soup to a stand blender or food processor in batches), purée the soup. For a fine texture, strain through a fine-mesh sieve.

2. Transfer the soup to serving bowls, garnish with the crème fraîche and mint leaves, and serve.

Coconut-Ginger Squash Soup with Peshwari Challah

serves 8

For years I enjoyed the old standard, butternut squash soup made with cider. Then, slurping a delicious Thai soup one day, I realised that Thai ingredients could bring squash soup to new heights. Thought to kitchen and here's the result – a marvellous soup brightened with fresh ginger and coconut milk, and served with Peshwari Challah, my naan-inspired bread with dried fruit, nuts and spices. You can serve this without the challah, but if you enjoy bread making, you must try it with.

1. In a food processor, combine the onion, celery, shallots and carrots, and pulse to chop.

2. In a large saucepan, heat the olive and grapeseed oils. Add the chopped mixture and sauté, stirring, until soft but not brown, about 10 minutes.

3. Add the squash and sauté, stirring often, until beginning to soften, about 15 minutes. (If using the squash purée, sauté for 5 minutes.)

4. Add the stock, coconut milk, cumin, turmeric, ginger and coriander stems. Bring to the boil, then reduce the heat and simmer until the squash is very soft, about 40 minutes. (For the squash purée, add and simmer for 20 minutes.) Remove the coriander.

5. Using a hand blender (or transferring the soup in batches to a standard blender), purée. Add the salt and pepper; adjust the seasoning, if necessary. Transfer to serving bowls, garnish with the chopped coriander, and serve with the challah, if desired.

Convert It

To make this meat, substitute chicken stock for the vegetable stock.

1 large onion, quartered

3 celery sticks, quartered

4 shallots, halved

2 medium carrots, quartered

2 tablespoons extra-virgin olive oil

2 tablespoons grapeseed or rapeseed oil

900g winter squash, cut into 5cm dice

950ml vegetable stock (page 193)

360ml light coconut milk

1 teaspoon ground cumin

½ teaspoon turmeric

1 teaspoon grated ginger

5 large stems coriander, washed, plus 20g chopped for garnish

1 teaspoon kosher salt

½ teaspoon freshly ground white pepper

Peshwari Challah (page 190) for serving (optional)

Fresh Vegetable Minestrone

serves 8–10

As wonderful as minestrone is, I'd never found it completely satisfying. Then I discovered the 'trick' of putting cheese rind in it. The rind adds body as well as flavour, making a great dish truly super. (For non-dairy versions, see Convert It.) Add some cooked ditalini or orzo and you've got a stick-to-the-ribs dish, which is perfect for cold weather. I also serve this as is to dieting friends – it's filling but low in calories.

Convert It

To make this a meat dish, substitute olive oil for the butter, chicken stock for the vegetable stock and omit the Parmesan. To make it pareve, use olive oil in place of the butter and omit the Parmesan.

2 tablespoons grapeseed or rapeseed oil

2 tablespoons butter

2 medium onions, finely sliced

2 garlic cloves, crushed with the side of a knife

1 large carrot, peeled and cut into 0.5cm dice

2 medium celery sticks, cut into 0.5cm dice

142g green beans, cut into 2.5cm pieces

2 medium courgettes, cut into 0.5cm dice

60g cabbage, finely sliced

2 x 400g tins peeled plum tomatoes, chopped into 1cm pieces, with their juice

700ml vegetable stock (page 193)

1 x 10cm rind Parmesan, or other hard, flavourful cheese, plus more grated for serving

285g chickpeas, drained and rinsed

kosher salt

1. Heat the oil and butter in a medium saucepan over a medium-high heat. When the foaming subsides, add the onion and garlic, and sauté, stirring, until translucent but not brown, about 8 minutes. Add the carrot and celery and sauté, stirring, until the vegetables begin to soften, about 3 minutes. Add the green beans, courgettes and cabbage, and sauté, stirring, until the vegetables begin to soften, about 5 minutes. Add the tomatoes with their juice and stir. Add the stock and rind, cover, reduce the heat and simmer for 1¹/2 hours.

2. Add the chickpeas and simmer for 20 minutes.

3. Remove the rind. Divide the soup among serving bowls, garnish with the grated Parmesan, season with salt and serve.

Four-Mushroom Onion Soup with Truffle Oil–Thyme Croûtes

serves 8–10

This complexly flavoured soup balances mushroom earthiness with the sweetness of caramelised onions, the woody taste of cognac and sophisticated truffle oil. It began with my discovery of sliced mixed mushrooms in my fridge. It was autumn and I was thinking onion soup. A bit of kitchen footwork and *voilà*. Well, almost. The addition of croûtes brushed with truffle oil adds to the dish's excitement. Truffle oil may sound la-di-da, but it's a great kitchen investment, something you'll use again and again, or you can substitute extra-virgin olive oil.

1. In a small bowl, combine the porcini mushrooms with 240ml of boiling water. Soak the mushrooms until soft, about 20 minutes.

2. Meanwhile, in a large, heavy saucepan, heat 3 tablespoons of the oil over a medium heat. Add the onions and sauté, stirring, until translucent, about 10 minutes. Reduce the heat to low, add the thyme and sauté, stirring occasionally, until the onions are golden-brown, about 30 minutes. Remove the thyme and set aside. Reserve the pan.

3. Strain the porcini, reserving the liquid, and chop the mushrooms coarsely. Place the saucepan over a medium-high heat and add the remaining oil. Add the porcini, white mushrooms, shiitakes and portobellos, and sauté, stirring, until the mushrooms are soft, about 8 minutes. Add the cognac, avert your face, then set aflame with a barbecue lighter or a lit tip of a wooden skewer. Add the garlic and sauté the mixture, 1–2 minutes. Add the wine and simmer until the liquid is reduced by half, about 5 minutes. Add the porcini liquid and 1.4 litres of the stock, then simmer to blend the flavours, 30–40 minutes.

4. Using a hand blender (or transferring the soup in batches to a stand blender), purée the soup. If the mixture seems too thick, add more stock. Add 3 tablespoons of the truffle oil in a thin stream and season with the salt and pepper.

5. Meanwhile, make the croûtes. Heat the oven to 170ºC/gas mark 3. In a small non-porous bowl combine the olive oil, 2 tablespoons of truffle oil and the thyme. Cover a baking sheet with foil and place the baguette slices on it. Brush with the oil mixture and bake until crisp, 12–15 minutes. Sprinkle with the salt.

6. Transfer the soup to serving bowls and garnish with the thyme and drops of the remaining truffle oil. Serve with the croûtes.

Convert It

To make this a pareve dish, use vegetable stock (page 193) in place of the chicken stock.

Geila's Tips

You can prepare the soup in advance and freeze it. If you do, don't add any additional stock or the truffle oil before freezing. To reheat the soup, allow it to thaw, then reheat it, adding stock as needed. Finish the soup with the oil.

30g dried porcini mushrooms

6 tablespoons grapeseed or rapeseed oil

3 large onions, finely sliced

3 thyme sprigs, plus more for garnish

340g shiitake mushrooms, stemmed and sliced 0.5cm thick

225g white mushrooms, sliced 0.5cm thick

350g portobello mushrooms, stemmed and sliced 0.5cm thick

60ml cognac

4 garlic cloves, finely chopped

240ml dry white wine

1.4–1.9 litres, as needed, chicken stock

6 tablespoons white truffle oil or extra-virgin olive oil, to taste

kosher salt and freshly ground black pepper

Croûtes

60ml extra-virgin olive oil

1 tablespoon chopped fresh thyme

12 x 0.5cm baguette slices

fleur de sel or kosher salt

chapter

4

Fish

Fish

Fresh, sweet fish is a canvas for creative cooking. So I'm often frustrated by the limited imagination many kosher cooks give it.

Because fish is pareve, it's usually served as an appetiser for a meat meal or as a main course for a dairy one. That's fine as far as traditional kosher practice goes, but we need to think more globally. There's much more to the kosher fish repertoire. Following the 'modern' approach, exciting fish dishes that were once off the table for kosher cooks are now at its centrepiece.

Thanks to the expanded kosher Asian store cupboard, kosher cooks can now prepare cutting-edge dishes like My Miso Glazed Black Cod, with its enticingly crisp, mirin- and miso-flavoured skin and melting flesh, and crunchy Pistachio-Crusted Tuna with Wasabi Mayonnaise. The expanded store cupboard is also key to haute cuisine-inspired dishes like Sea Bass with Black Bean Beurre Blanc, and Sole-Wrapped Asparagus with Hollandaise, a dish that should put that luscious sauce on your kitchen map.

A lot of what's wonderful about seafood can be replicated in kosher dishes. Surimi, a fish-based product that comes in a variety of shellfish flavours, works beautifully in Surimi Crab Cakes with Red Pepper Mayonnaise. These were once a no-go for kosher cooks and diners, but no longer. Another conversion approach is to substitute firm, sweet-fleshed fish for the shellfish, or, if possible, eliminate the shellfish entirely. My version of the wonderful French fish stew Bourride with Aioli does both. It features toothsome fish that provides seafood texture while dispensing with the shellfish that's usually included in the traditional dish. It also shows you how a dish can be thickened with an oil and egg-yolk emulsion – the aioli, a mayonnaise – instead of dairy products.

Sometimes all that's needed to make a dish kosher is a meat-to-fish switch. Salmon with Creamed Leeks simply uses poached salmon in place of the traditional chicken to make a dish that's creamy yet meatless. What's 'modern' about this dish, and all the others in this chapter, is a way of thinking. When you expand your sense of what's possible, you free your imagination to create exciting fish dishes where once there were none.

Salmon with Creamed Leeks

serves 6

This delicious dish gives you all the thrills of French cooking without any of the hassle. You poach salmon partly off the heat - a foolproof technique that's unattended and ensures perfect doneness. The creamy leek bed is equally easy to do, but you can make it, and even the salmon, in advance (see Tip). The finished dish is great for company, and gets applause every time.

1. In a large sauté pan, heat the butter and oil over a medium heat. Add the leeks and season with the salt. Reduce the heat to medium-low and sauté until translucent, stirring occasionally, about 10 minutes.

2. Add the wine, bring to the boil and cook until the wine has evaporated, about 3 minutes. Add the cream, dill and cumin, and simmer until lightly thickened, about 10 minutes. The mixture should coat a spoon lightly. Season with pepper and adjust the salt, if necessary.

3. Add the poaching liquid ingredients to a sauté pan large enough to hold the fillets in a single layer. Add enough water to bring the liquid 1cm from the top of the pan. Add the fillet skin side down and bring the liquid to the boil. Reduce the heat to low and barely simmer the fillets for 5 minutes. Turn the fillets, remove the pan from the heat, and remove their skin. By the time the liquid has cooled, the fillets will be done.

4. Transfer the leek mixture to a warmed platter. Using a slotted spatula, transfer the fish to the platter atop the leeks. Serve.

Geila's Tip

You can prepare the leek mixture a day in advance, refrigerate it and, just before you poach the fish, reheat it over a low heat, adding additional cream, if needed. If you want to make the fish in advance too, poach and refrigerate it, then bring it to room temperature, or heat it in a low oven.

---

2 tablespoons unsalted butter

2 tablespoons grapeseed or rapeseed oil

5 medium leeks (about 900g) white parts only, well washed and sliced 1cm thick

salt and freshly ground black pepper

120ml white wine

360 ml double or single cream

3 tablespoons chopped dill

½ teaspoon cumin

Poaching Liquid

240ml white wine

4 peppercorns

4 large dill sprigs

½ teaspoon kosher salt

6 salmon fillets (about 1.3kg), 4-5cm thick

Bourride with Aïoli

serves 4-6

I miss bouillabaisse, which usually contains shellfish. When I discovered bourride, a creamy, garlicky French fish stew that's equally satisfying, I was overjoyed. The stew's richness – and pungency – is supplied by garlic-laced aïoli, a Mediterranean mayonnaise that you add to the stew *and* serve with it. This is a great pareve dish, as its texture suggests that cream has been added, but there's none in it.

You can prepare the aïoli ahead, refrigerating it, then bringing it to room temperature before adding it to the stew. The aïoli contains uncooked egg yolks; always use the freshest eggs you can buy from reliable sources, or use pasteurised eggs. Ask your fishmonger for the fish bones and skin, but if you can't get them, do without. The stew will still taste wonderful.

Geila's Tips

Always use a non-porous bowl when preparing the aïoli. Metals such as aluminium can darken it. If the aïoli breaks or curdles while you're making it, place an egg yolk in a clean bowl and beat it. Beating, add the curdled mixture in drops. Increase the amount added until the mixture has emulsified and thickened.

You can swap unskinned boiled potatoes for the baguette. Place in serving bowls before adding the soup.

Aïoli

½ teaspoon saffron threads (optional)

240ml fruity extra-virgin olive oil

120ml rapeseed oil

8 garlic cloves

1 teaspoon kosher salt

4 egg yolks from large eggs

¼ teaspoon white pepper

juice ½ lemon

Bourride

2 tablespoons extra-virgin olive oil, plus more for brushing

1 tablespoon grapeseed or rapeseed oil

5 garlic cloves, finely chopped

1 medium onion, chopped

2 leeks, white part only, well washed (see Tip, page 54), chopped

1 sprig thyme

1 fennel bulb, sliced 0.5cm thick (see Tip, page 84)

1 teaspoon kosher salt

1. First make the aïoli. In a small bowl, combine the saffron threads, if using, with 1 tablespoon of warm water. Allow to soak until the saffron has softened, about 10 minutes. Strain the saffron and set aside. In a measuring jug, combine the oils. In a medium bowl, crush the garlic with the salt. Transfer to the bowl of an electric mixer fitted with the whisk attachment. Add the yolks, pepper and saffron, if using, and beat on medium speed until the yolks have thickened. Without stopping the mixer, add the oils drop by drop. After 60ml has been added, add the oils slowly in a narrow stream. When the aïoli becomes thick, stop adding the oils and beat in the lemon juice and 1 tablespoon of hot water to stabilise and thin it slightly. (If the mixture breaks, see Tip.) Transfer half of the aïoli to a non-porous serving bowl, cover and refrigerate. Leave the remaining aïoli in the mixing bowl.

2. To make the bourride, in a medium saucepan, heat the oils over a medium heat. Add the garlic, onion, leeks, thyme and fennel. Season with the salt and sauté, stirring, until the vegetables have softened but not browned, about 10 minutes. Add the tomatoes, saffron, wine and 950ml of water, increase the heat and bring to the boil. Add the fish bones and skin, if using, reduce the heat and simmer for 20 minutes. Add the fish, push it gently under the liquid, and poach at a bare simmer until the fish is just cooked through, about 10 minutes. With a slotted spoon, transfer the fish to a bowl large enough to hold it, and keep warm. Strain the bourride into a large, clean saucepan.

3. Meanwhile heat the oven to 180°C/gas mark 4. Place the bread onto a baking tray, brush with olive oil, and toast, turning, until the bread is crisp, about 5 minutes. Keep warm.

4. Using a hand mixer on medium speed, whisk the egg yolks into the aioli in the mixing bowl. Continuing to whisk, slowly transfer the bourride to the aioli in the mixing bowl, and when blended, return to the saucepan. Stirring constantly, gently reheat the bourride to thicken the soup to a thin custard consistency, about 7 minutes. Do not allow the bourride to simmer or boil, or it will curdle.

5. Bring the reserved aioli to room temperature. Divide the fish and bread among large serving bowls, ladle the soup over and serve with the aioli. Alternatively, dollop the aioli onto the bread and serve with the soup.

2 x 400g tins peeled plum tomatoes, roughly chopped

¼ teaspoon saffron threads, crushed

240ml white wine

1.3kg firm white fish, such as snapper, grouper or sea bass, or a mixture, cut into 5cm cubes, plus bones and skin (if available), rinsed

1 baguette, cut diagonally into 12–16 slices

2 egg yolks from large eggs, beaten

Surimi Crab Cakes with Red Pepper Mayonnaise

serves 4 as main, 8 as a starter

For a long time after I returned to kosher eating, I really missed crab cakes, which were one of my favourite foods, especially in summer. When I was introduced to surimi crab sticks, I jumped for joy. The surimi has the sweet and salty flavour of crab, and works beautifully in these lightly fried cakes. Serve these with Sweetcorn Salad (page 137) and sliced avocado in addition to the mayo, and you've got yourself a feast.

Geila's Tips

To make fresh breadcrumbs, remove the crusts from 4 slices of white bread, and pulse in a food processor until small crumbs are formed.

Formed to make cakes about 3cm in diameter, these make wonderful hors d'oeuvres.

340g seafood sticks, see Store Cupboard, page 19

1½ teaspoons Old Bay seasoning

2 tablespoons mayonnaise

10g chopped coriander or flat-leaf parsley

25g fresh breadcrumbs (see Tip)

1 medium egg, beaten

1 teaspoon mustard

3 spring onions, white parts, finely sliced

25g roasted red pepper (see step 3, page 48), cut into 0.5cm dice

kosher salt and freshly ground black pepper

30g panko

2 tablespoons grapeseed or rapeseed oil

Red Pepper Mayonnaise (page 197), for serving

1. In a medium bowl, combine the surimi, Old Bay seasoning, mayonnaise, coriander, breadcrumbs, egg, mustard, spring onion and red pepper, and mix. Season with the salt and pepper, and blend. Transfer to the fridge and chill for 1 hour.

2. Form four 8cm patties with the mixture and transfer them to a flat dish. Spread the panko on a second dish and gently coat the cakes on all sides with the crumbs, returning the cakes to the first dish when formed. Chill the breaded cakes for at least 1 hour or overnight.

3. Heat the oil in a large frying pan over a medium-high heat until hot but not smoking. Add the cakes and sauté, turning once, until golden brown, 6–10 minutes. Drain the cakes on kitchen paper, transfer to plates and serve with the Red Pepper Mayonnaise.

My Miso-Glazed Black Cod

serves 6

New York's Nobu restaurant, 1985: chef Nobu Matsuhisa's miso-glazed black cod. Me on first taste: *wow!* I longed to make a kosher version of this great dish, but had to bide my time until kosher miso became available. On that happy day I set to work – and here it is, a dish you'll enjoy often and that's super easy to make. All you do is marinate black cod in a simple miso-sugar mixture then grill or barbecue it. The caramelised skin is delightfully crispy, and really complements the sweet, moist flesh. Served over sautéd spinach and with a side of mashed potatoes – or on its own with any bitter green – this is stellar dining.

Geila's Tips

This also makes an elegant starter. Just reduce the portion size by half and serve the cod on greens lightly dressed with Asian Vinaigrette (page 32).

I also use this glaze brushed on aubergine when I grill it. Serve the aubergine with roasted meat.

120ml mirin

120ml sake or dry white wine

280g white miso

130g sugar

6 black cod fillets (170–225g each), skin removed (if you can't find black cod, use any other firm white fish)

1. In a medium heavy-based saucepan, combine the mirin and sake, and bring to the boil. Boil for 1 minute (to cook off the alcohol), reduce the heat to medium, add the miso and stir until dissolved. Add the sugar, increase the heat and stir until the sugar is dissolved, about 5 minutes. Remove from the heat and cool to room temperature.

2. Dry the fillets with kitchen paper and put them in a large sealable freezer bag. Add the miso glaze, seal and refrigerate for 24–48 hours.

3. Bring the fillets to room temperature. Preheat the grill, or place a griddle pan or heavy frying pan over a high heat. Wipe excess glaze from the fillets and grill or fry, turning once, until brown and glazed, about 8 minutes. Transfer to plates and serve.

Sea Bass with Black Bean Beurre Blanc

serves 8

I was a great fan of Chinese steamed fish with black beans – and of beurre blanc, that creamy French sauce that sounds troublesome to make, but isn't. Here, one of my favourite fish is paired with a black bean-flavoured beurre blanc, a terrific marriage. You could use another white fish, but the sea bass really complements the sauce, and vice versa. I serve this with wilted greens and a frizzled-leek garnish, but it's great with any simple accompaniment.

Geila's Tips

The fish and the sauce can be prepared ahead of time. The sauce will hold at room temperature for up to 3 hours over warm water, or transfer it to a thermos, where it will stay warm for 5 hours or longer. Transfer the sautéed fish to a baking sheet lined with parchment paper. Cover lightly with foil and leave on the counter. For serving, reheat the fish in a 200°C/gas mark 6 oven for 4 minutes and serve with the sauce.

Beurre blanc

225g unsalted butter

2 medium shallots, finely chopped

1 teaspoon white wine vinegar or unseasoned rice wine vinegar

360ml dry white wine

120ml sake

3 tablespoons chopped, rinsed and dried fermented black beans

2 thyme sprigs

2 tablespoons double cream

kosher salt and freshly ground black pepper

Fish

1 tablespoon unsalted butter

1 tablespoon grapeseed or rapeseed oil

8 x 170–225g sea bass fillets, skin and bloodlines removed

kosher salt and freshly ground black pepper

1. First make the beurre blanc. In a heavy medium saucepan, melt 1 tablespoon of the butter over a medium heat. Add the shallots and sauté, stirring, until soft but not brown, about 2 minutes. Add the vinegar, wine, sake, black beans and thyme, and reduce by two-thirds, 6–8 minutes. Add the cream and reduce the mixture until thick, about 3 minutes. Turn the heat to very low and whisk in the remaining butter, adding first 1 tablespoon and then 2 tablespoons at a time, until a light emulsion is formed. If the butter gives any indication of melting, remove the pan from the hob. Season with salt and pepper, and keep warm.

2. In a large frying pan, heat the butter and oil over a medium-high heat. Season the fillets on both sides with salt and pepper. When the butter has stopped foaming, and working in batches, gently transfer the fillets, without crowding, to the pan. Sauté, carefully turning once, until golden brown, about 8 minutes. (If the fish is more than 2.5cm thick, sauté for 10 minutes.) Transfer the fish to plates, spoon some of the beurre blanc over each portion, and serve with the remaining sauce.

Sole-Wrapped Asparagus with Hollandaise

serves 6

Here's a classic pairing – a couple of them, in fact. Asparagus and hollandaise is one of those matches made in heaven, as is sole served with the sauce. People sometimes avoid hollandaise, fearing its richness or the possibility of it 'breaking' while they make it. With my quick, foolproof method, hollandaise will become an indispensable sauce in your house. The presentation – the asparagus is wrapped in sole fillets and baked – is also easily done, and looks beautiful.

1. Preheat the oven to 200ºC/gas mark 6. Fill a large bowl with cold water and add ice. Bring a large saucepan of salted water to the boil, add the asparagus and cook until bright green, 1-2 minutes, depending on the type. Using tongs or a slotted spatula, transfer the asparagus to the ice bath. When cold, drain on kitchen paper.

2. Grease a large baking dish with 1 tablespoon of the butter. Bunch 4-6 asparagus spears and wrap with a fillet. Repeat with the remaining asparagus and fillets. Transfer to the baking dish seam side down, and sprinkle with the salt, pepper and tarragon. Pour the wine into the bottom of the dish, dot the fish bundles with the remaining tablespoon of butter, and bake until the fish is barely cooked through, about 15 minutes. (The fish will continue to cook away from the heat.) Remove from the oven and leave to rest for 5 minutes.

3. Meanwhile, make the hollandaise. In a small frying pan, melt the butter without browning over a medium-low heat. This can also be done in a glass measuring jug in the microwave, stopping and stirring every 15 seconds until the butter is melted. If melting the butter on the hob, transfer the butter to a small measuring jug with a spout.

4. In a 500ml measuring jug (or a hand-blender beaker), combine the egg yolks, cayenne, salt and double cream then, using a hand blender, beat until the mixture begins to thicken, 45 seconds to 1 minute. While beating, gradually add the melted butter. After half the butter has been added, and the mixture has begun to thicken, beat in the lemon juice and the salt, and add the remaining butter. Alternatively, make the sauce using an ordinary blender. Adjust the seasoning, if necessary.

5. Transfer the fish to warmed serving plates, spoon the sauce over the fish and serve.

Fish

24 medium, or 36 fine, asparagus spears, trimmed

2 tablespoons unsalted butter

6 x 170-225g sole fillets, trimmed, rinsed and dried

1 teaspoon kosher salt

12 teaspoons white pepper

2 tablespoons finely chopped fresh tarragon leaves, or 2 teaspoons dried

120ml white wine

Hollandaise

225g unsalted butter

4 egg yolks from large eggs, at room temperature

⅛ teaspoon cayenne

1 tablespoon double cream

2 tablespoons fresh lemon juice

1 teaspoon kosher salt, plus more if needed

Pistachio-Crusted Tuna with Wasabi Mayonnaise

serves 4

My Passover shopping usually takes me to Manhattan's Lower East Side. One year my eyes were bigger than my stomach, and I bought more pistachios than I needed. When I discovered the 'extra' nuts I'd stored in my freezer, I immediately thought *tuna with a crunchy pistachio coating*, and this dish was soon born. It's easy to make. The fish is quickly marinated – or you can marinate it overnight, in which case it's super quick to prepare. Served with tongue-tingling wasabi mayonnaise, this works equally well for company and weeknight dining.

Geila's Tip

I like my tuna rare. If you prefer yours cooked through, bake rather than sauté the fish in a 175°C oven for about 15 minutes.

680g tuna steak, cut into 4 x 4cm cubes

2 tablespoons soy sauce

3 tablespoons mirin, or 2 tablespoons white wine mixed with 2 tablespoons sugar

½ teaspoon wasabi powder

5 tablespoons grapeseed or rapeseed oil

100g finely chopped unsalted pistachios

Wasabi Mayonnaise (page 197), for serving

1. Place the tuna in a large freezer bag. In a 500ml measuring jug (or a hand-blender beaker), combine the soy sauce, mirin, wasabi and 2 tablespoons of the oil, and blend using a hand blender. Alternatively, blend in an ordinary blender. Pour the mixture into the bag with the tuna, and marinate the fish for at least 30 minutes at room temperature, or overnight in the fridge.

2. Distribute the pistachios on a large plate. One at a time, remove the tuna from the bag, shake off excess marinade, and roll in the pistachios so that all sides are coated. Set aside.

3. In a large frying pan, heat the remaining 3 tablespoons of oil over a medium-high heat. Transfer the tuna to the pan and sauté, giving the fish a quarter-turn every 45 seconds, until the tuna is seared and rare inside. Do not allow the nuts to burn. Transfer the tuna to a chopping board, cover with foil, and leave to rest for 3 minutes.

4. Slice the tuna about 0.5cm thick. Fan the tuna on serving plates and drizzle with the mayonnaise, or serve the mayonnaise on the side.

chapter

5

Poultry

Poultry

Whaen people ask me where my dish ideas come from, I tell them I look first to the world's best recipes – and they should too. Adapt them using your 'modern toolbox', and you'll create terrific kosher food.

For example, Chicken with Sausage, Fennel and Peas is an almost word-for-word translation of the traditional Italian pasta dish featuring those ingredients minus the chicken. Kosher cooks can now make it by using newly available kosher sausage. The sausage also adds savour to the stuffing accompaniment to High-Heat Roast Turkey, a dish that in itself relies on the availability of small, freshly killed kosher turkeys for its cooking ease. And the bird's gravy is enticingly enhanced by the addition of kosher port, an ingredient that, together with kosher duck breasts, makes possible a kosher version of the delicious French classic Duck Breast with Port and Figs. That dish came about when a food-loving friend expressed a wish for a French speciality that was also kosher.

Some adaptations blend traditions. The cross-cultural Asian Coleslaw with Chicken salutes American coleslaw dishes, but relies for its tempting dressing on soy and sesame oil, and on crushed dry ramen noodles for crunchy texture.

My take on the French Poulet Véronique, Chicken with Grapes and Mushrooms, is now an everyday classic. Incidentally, it was also my first kosher-dish adaptation, created at college. Back then there was no kosher dry white wine and I had to make do with vinegar. Now we can use the real thing.

I've also included Cinnamon Chicken Tagine with Prunes and Apricots, a deeply satisfying dish of the Jewish diaspora. It's passed through many hands over the years. Now you have my version.

Sometimes thinking outside the box means thinking close to home. Baked Herbed Chicken is an American classic, a savoury, easy-to-do family dish that's stood the test of time. I think of it as a menu building block, a foundation recipe that will help you establish a repertoire of simple specialities, the result, I hope, of your own 'modern' smartness.

Chicken with Sausage, Fennel and Peas

serves 6-8

I love fresh fennel, a vegetable that the Italians dote on but that we tend to neglect. Paired here with chicken and sausage – a great combo in itself – the vegetable really shines. This one-pot dish, perfect for family dining or casual entertaining, owes its existence to newly improved Italian-style kosher sausage. Don't let the number of ingredients put you off; everything goes together quickly, and the result pleases everybody.

Geila's Tips

To slice the fennel easily, trim the stalks from the bulb, and halve it top to bottom. Core and place each half on a chopping board and slice it across as you would an onion.

You can prepare steps 1-7 several hours in advance. Reheat the dish in a 190°C oven and proceed.

6 tablespoons rapeseed oil, plus more if needed

450g sweet Italian sausage (page 19), sliced 2.5cm thick

65g plain flour

12 chicken thighs

7 tablespoons olive oil, plus more if needed

1 large fennel bulb, finely sliced

kosher salt

2 large onions, finely sliced

12 garlic cloves

340g Anja potatoes, peeled and cut into 4cm pieces

2 small lemons

240ml chicken stock

240ml white wine

3 rosemary sprigs

4 fresh sage leaves

3 tablespoons fresh oregano or 1 tablespoon dried

250g frozen peas, defrosted

1. Preheat the oven to 190°C/gas mark 5.

2. In a large sauté pan, heat 2 tablespoons of the rapeseed oil over a medium heat. Add the sausage and sauté, turning once, until brown, about 5 minutes. Transfer the sausage to a roasting pan and reserve the first pan.

3. Meanwhile, spread the flour on a large plate, add the chicken and dredge it. Heat 2 tablespoons each of the olive and rapeseed oil in the pan over a medium heat. Shake excess flour from the chicken, add it to the pan and sauté, turning once, until brown, 8-10 minutes. Transfer the chicken to the roasting pan.

4. If the flour has blackened, wash the pan and add 2 tablespoons each of the rapeseed and olive oils. Otherwise, pour off half of the remaining oil from the pan. Heat over a medium heat, add the fennel, season with salt and sauté, stirring, until the fennel has wilted, 5-7 minutes. Add the onions and sauté over a medium heat, stirring, until soft, about 8 minutes. Season with salt and transfer the vegetables to the roasting pan.

5. In the same pan, combine 3 tablespoons of the olive oil, the garlic, the potatoes and 240ml of water. Bring to the boil and cook until the liquid has evaporated and the potatoes begin to colour in the oil, 12-15 minutes. Transfer to the roasting pan. (The potatoes won't be cooked through.)

6. Squeeze the lemon over the roasting pan mixture, add the stock, wine, rosemary, sage and oregano, and bake until juices run clear when the chicken is pierced with the point of a knife or the internal temperature reaches 70°C, 30-45 minutes.

7. Transfer the chicken, sausage and potatoes, plus any larger pieces of onion and fennel, to a warmed platter. Add the peas to the pan and warm in residual heat, stirring, about 2 minutes. Pour the peas and pan sauce over the platter mixture and serve.

High-Heat Roast Turkey with Apple, Cranberry and Sausage Stuffing

servers 10–12

My mother never believes that a turkey can be roasted to succulent perfection in about two hours, and declares it a miracle every time the 'miraculous' occurs. I just smile – and you will too, when you try this fast, easy method. The 'trick' is to use a 5–6kg bird, which is ample for most turkey-roasting occasions. The stuffing, rich with tart fruit and sausage, is always praised too, as is the port-laced gravy.

Geila's Tip

I like to put the turkey seasoning mixture under the skin (in addition to rubbing it on and inside the bird) before roasting it. To do this, just work your fingers between the skin and flesh at both neck and tail ends, and rub in the mixture.

Stuffing

6 tablespoons grapeseed or rapeseed oil

100g pine nuts

450g sweet Italian sausage, casings removed (page 202)

230g chopped onions

4 garlic cloves, crushed with the flat of a knife

5 shallots, chopped

3 Granny Smith apples, peeled, cored and cut into 0.5cm dice

2 celery sticks, chopped

2 tablespoons chopped thyme

180ml white wine

240ml organic apple juice

65g dried cranberries

450g stale bread, cut into 0.5cm cubes

1 large egg, beaten

240–480ml chicken stock, as needed

vegetable oil, for greasing

kosher salt and freshly ground black pepper

fat drippings from the roasted turkey

Turkey

1 x 5–6kg fresh turkey, neck reserved

480ml fresh chicken stock

115g margarine, melted

1. First make the stuffing. Heat 1 tablespoon of the oil in a large sauté pan over a low heat. Add the pine nuts and sauté, stirring, until fragrant, 3–4 minutes. Remove and reserve. Add the sausage and sauté, breaking it up, until brown, about 10 minutes. Add a little water while the sausage cooks to help break up the meat.

2. Add 3 tablespoons of the oil to the pan and heat over a medium-high heat. Add the onions, garlic and shallots, and sauté, stirring, until translucent, 5–7 minutes. Add the apples, celery, and remaining oil, and sauté, stirring, until they have begun to soften, 3–4 minutes. Add the thyme, wine and cider, and stir. Add the cranberries, reduce the heat to low and cook until the liquid has evaporated, about 12 minutes. Add the pine nuts and stir. Transfer to a large bowl, add the bread and toss. Add the egg and 240ml of the stock, and stir gently. If the stuffing seems dry, drizzle in more stock and blend lightly.

3. Preheat the oven to 180ºC/gas mark 4. Coat a large baking dish with vegetable oil, add the stuffing and cover with foil. Bake the stuffing for 45 minutes, remove the foil and bake until the surface is crisp, about 15 minutes. Set aside in a warm place.

4. To cook the turkey, preheat the oven to 200ºC/gas mark 6. Place a rack in a roasting pan and spray the rack with non-stick cooking spray. Add the turkey neck, stock and 120ml of water to the bottom of the pan.

5. Place the margarine in a small bowl. Add the sage, salt and pepper, blend, and massage the turkey inside and out with the mixture. Place the bird, breast side down, on the rack and roast for 20 minutes. Give the turkey a quarter-turn so one side faces up, and roast for 20 minutes more. Rotate the bird in the opposite direction so the other side faces up, and roast for 20 minutes. Rotate again so the breast faces up. If the breast seems to be browning too quickly, place a foil tent over it. The turkey is done when a thermometer inserted between the thigh and the body registers 70ºC. Transfer the turkey to a chopping board and leave to rest for 15 minutes. Reserve the roasting pan.

6. To make the gravy, in a small frying pan, melt the margarine over a medium-low heat. Add the flour and cook, stirring, until the roux is caramel coloured, about 8 minutes. Watch carefully as the mixture can burn quickly. Remove the pan from the hob and set aside.

7. Pour off the fat from the roasting pan and place the pan over the hob. Heat over a medium-high heat, add the port and deglaze the pan. Add enough stock to make 480ml of liquid and whisk in half of the roux. Simmer until the gravy thickens, 4-5 minutes. If the gravy seems too thin, whisk in more of the roux, and simmer. If the gravy seems too thick, whisk in more stock.

8. Run hot water through a metal sieve to heat it, and strain the gravy into a gravy boat. Carve the turkey and serve with the gravy and stuffing.

8-10 sage leaves, finely chopped

1 tablespoon kosher salt

1 teaspoon freshly ground black pepper

Gravy

2 tablespoons margarine

3 tablespoons plain flour

60ml port or Madeira

480-600ml chicken stock, as needed

Baked Herb Chicken
serves 6

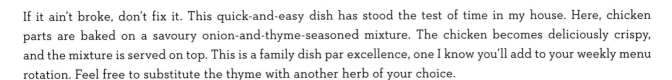

If it ain't broke, don't fix it. This quick-and-easy dish has stood the test of time in my house. Here, chicken parts are baked on a savoury onion-and-thyme-seasoned mixture. The chicken becomes deliciously crispy, and the mixture is served on top. This is a family dish par excellence, one I know you'll add to your weekly menu rotation. Feel free to substitute the thyme with another herb of your choice.

1. Preheat the oven to 200ºC/gas mark 6.

2. In a large roasting pan, combine the onions, garlic and thyme. Sprinkle with the salt, add the olive oil and toss. Lay the chicken on top, skin side down, and sprinkle with the lemon juice. Bake for 30 minutes, turn, and bake until cooked through, 15-20 minutes. If pricked with a fork the juices should run clear, or cook to an internal temperature of 70ºC. If the skin isn't crisp, transfer the chicken to the grill and brown, 3-5 minutes.

3. Transfer the chicken to a platter, return the pan to the oven, and bake until the onions have caramelised and the juice is reduced, about 20 minutes. Remove the thyme, spoon the onion mixture over the chicken, and serve.

2 large onions, finely sliced

4 garlic cloves, crushed with the side of a knife

8 sprigs thyme

1 teaspoon salt

3 tablespoons extra-virgin olive oil

12 chicken thighs, bone in, skin on, rinsed, dried well and excess fat removed

juice 1 lemon

Duck Breast with Port and Figs

serves 6

Several years ago, the French husband of a friend who keeps kosher bemoaned the lack of kosher haute cuisine. So for his birthday I 'gave' him this delicious dish. It's definitely high quality, but also easy to do. Duck breasts with port and figs is one of those meant-to-be combinations. This will *make* your next special dinner, I promise.

1. In a small saucepan, heat the oil over a medium-high heat. Add the shallots and sauté, stirring, until translucent, about 4 minutes. Add the garlic and sauté for 3 minutes. Add the port, stock, all the figs and thyme. Bring to the boil, reduce the heat and simmer until the liquid turns to syrup, about 1 minute. With a slotted spoon, remove the halved figs and set aside. Strain the sauce, pressing on the solids, and set aside.

2. Preheat the oven to 200ºC/gas mark 6. Heat a large frying pan over a medium-high heat. Add the breasts skin side down and cook without moving until the skin is crisp and the fat rendered, about 6 minutes. Drain the fat, reserving it for another use.

3. Season the breasts with salt and pepper, turn over, and transfer the pan to the oven. Roast until the breasts are medium rare, about 6 minutes, or 10 minutes for medium. Transfer the breasts to a chopping board, cover lightly with foil and leave to rest for 10 minutes.

4. Slice the breasts diagonally and divide among warmed serving plates. Spoon the sauce over them, garnish each with the fig halves and serve.

Geila's Tip

The sauce can be made a day in advance and stored, covered, in the fridge. If you want a super-deluxe dish, use veal stock instead of chicken stock.

---

2 tablespoons grapeseed or rapeseed oil

68g finely chopped shallots

1 garlic clove, crushed with the side of a knife

240ml ruby port

360ml chicken stock

12 large fresh figs, 6 finely chopped, 6 halved

2 sprigs thyme

6 x 225g duck breasts, rinsed, dried, excess fat removed, skin scored in a diamond pattern

kosher salt and freshly ground black pepper

Cinnamon Chicken Tagine with Prunes and Apricots

serves 10–12

Most cooks know that tagines are sweet and savoury dishes, usually featuring chicken, made in an earthenware cooking dish with a tall conical lid. My version honours traditional Jewish Moroccan tagines, but without the need of a special pot. Flavoured with cinnamon, and full of sweet fruit, this is a perfect celebration dish, especially good for Rosh Hashanah, Passover and Tu Bishvat. It's a great weekend family dish too.

Geila's Tip

This makes a large quantity, perfect for gatherings, but can be halved for fewer diners, or freeze half for later.

40g flaked almonds

2 chickens, about 1.6kg each, each cut into 8 pieces, or 16 breasts, thighs and legs, any combination, rinsed and dried well

kosher salt and freshly ground pepper

¼ cup grapeseed or rapeseed oil

2 large onions, cut into 1cm dice

½ teaspoon saffron threads, ground, powdered or crushed

480ml chicken stock

2 cinnamon sticks, each about 7.5cm long

265g pitted prunes

150g dried apricots

4 tablespoons honey

1. Heat a large frying pan, paella pan or large roasting pan, set on the hob over a medium-high heat. Add the almonds and toast, stirring, until lightly coloured, about 3 minutes. Transfer to a small bowl and set aside.

2. Sprinkle the chicken with salt and pepper. Heat half of the oil in the pan over a medium heat. Working in batches, add the chicken and sauté until brown, turning once, about 12 minutes per batch. Transfer to a large plate and set aside. If the oil or browned bits in the pan have burned, wipe out the pan.

3. Add the remaining oil to the pan. Add the onions and sauté, stirring, until the onions are translucent, about 10 minutes. Return the chicken to the pan. Add the saffron to the stock and pour over the chicken. Add the cinnamon, bring to the boil, reduce the heat, cover and simmer for 30 minutes. Transfer the white meat to the plate. Add the prunes and apricots to the pan and simmer until the rest of the chicken is done, about 15 minutes. Transfer the chicken to the plate and discard the cinnamon sticks.

4. Add the honey to the pan and cook over a medium-high heat until the liquid is syrupy and coats a spoon, 15–20 minutes. Return the chicken to the pan, baste with the sauce, cover and warm. Transfer all to a warmed platter, sprinkle with the almonds and serve.

Asian Coleslaw with Chicken

serves 6

Traditional, mayo-based coleslaws often miss the mark. This main-dish coleslaw with grilled chicken gets a savoury Asian spin with the addition of a soy sauce- and sesame oil-based dressing. Almonds and crushed ramen noodles – a garnish to keep in mind for other uses – add texture and crunch. I prefer flavourful dark meat for this, but feel free to use white. Fresh cabbage is first choice, but you can use shop-bought coleslaw for convenience. Minus the chicken, this makes a delicious side. You can make this in advance; just dress directly before serving.

Geila's Tips

To crush the ramen noodles, place them in a resealable plastic bag, seal, and roll a heavy tin over them.

Convert It

To make this pareve, eliminate the chicken. The dish works equally well for non-meat-eaters.

Marinade

60ml mirin

2 tablespoons toasted sesame oil

2 tablespoons soy sauce

3 garlic cloves, crushed

60ml sake or dry white wine

½ teaspoon kosher salt

60ml rapeseed oil

1.2kg boneless skinless chicken thighs or breasts

80g flaked almonds

45g sesame seeds

85g ramen noodles, crushed

Dressing

50g sugar

60ml mirin

3 tablespoons toasted sesame oil

2 tablespoons soy sauce

120ml rice vinegar

240ml grapeseed or rapeseed oil

1 medium head Chinese cabbage, finely sliced, or 285g ready-made coleslaw

6 spring onions, white parts only, finely sliced

1. In a large sealable freezer bag, combine the marinade ingredients. Add the chicken, press out any air from the bag, seal and refrigerate overnight.

2. Heat a medium sauté pan over a medium heat. Add the almonds and toast until golden, stirring to prevent burning, about 5 minutes. Transfer to a bowl. In the same pan, toast the noodles until golden, stirring, about 8 minutes, and transfer to the bowl. Toast the sesame seeds in the pan, stirring, until golden, about 8 minutes, and transfer to the bowl. Set aside. (You can make this beforehand. If you do, cool it completely, transfer it to a lidded container and store it at room temperature.)

3. Heat a large griddle pan or heavy frying pan over a medium heat. Add the marinated chicken, shaking off excess marinade, and gently fry until just cooked through, turning once, about 12 minutes for breasts, 15 minutes for thighs. Alternatively, grill, turning once, until just cooked through, or cook on a barbecue, 12-15 minutes. Transfer the chicken to a chopping board, cool and cut into bite-sized pieces.

4. To make the dressing, in a medium bowl, combine all the ingredients except the oil. Using a hand blender or whisk, blend, adding the oil in a steady stream until the mixture has thickened.

5. In a large bowl, combine the chicken, almonds, sesame seeds, ramen, coleslaw and spring onions. Just before serving, drizzle in the dressing and toss. Transfer to individual plates and serve.

Chicken with Grapes and Mushrooms

serves 4

This was my first 'wow' dish, invented while I was at college. I'd have at least ten guests to dinner on Friday nights, and I remember the pleasure of hearing the usual rambunctious crowd go silent after tasting it. They loved my cooking! The dish remains a family- and crowd-pleaser, enjoyed by kids and adults alike. A simple 'bake', you can serve it straight from the oven, warm or cold. And it's flexible. I've made it with a great variety of white-flour crackers, both plain and seasoned, whatever's in the house, and the dish scores every time.

1. On a large plate or in a shallow bowl, combine the crumbs, tarragon, 1½ teaspoons salt and ¼ teaspoon white pepper, and spread evenly. Add the chicken and dredge on both sides.

2. In a large frying pan, heat 1 tablespoon of the olive oil and 2 tablespoons of the grapeseed oil over a medium-high heat. Add the chicken and sauté, turning once, until brown, about 6 minutes. Transfer to a large baking dish.

3. Preheat the oven to 180ºC/gas mark 4. Wipe out the frying pan and heat the remaining grapeseed oil over a medium-high heat. Add the onion, sprinkle with a little salt (to help it release its moisture) and sauté, stirring, until translucent, about 4 minutes. Add 120ml of the wine and 120ml of the stock, bring to the boil to deglaze the pan, and pour over the chicken. Bake the chicken for 10 minutes.

4. Meanwhile, heat the remaining olive oil and grapeseed oil in the frying pan over a medium-high heat. Add the mushrooms, sprinkle with salt, and sauté until tender and golden, 4–5 minutes. Add the remaining wine and stock, and boil until almost all of the liquid has evaporated, 2–3 minutes. Add the grapes, stir and transfer to the baking dish. Bake the chicken until just cooked through, about 10 minutes.

5. Transfer the chicken to serving plates, spoon the sauce, grapes and mushrooms over it, and serve.

Geila's Tips

If I'm buying crackers for this, I get Manischewitz Tam Tam Crackers.

To make the crumbs, pulse whole crackers in a food processor.

150g cracker crumbs, any kind (see headnote and Tips)

2 teaspoons dried tarragon

1½ teaspoons kosher salt, plus more

¼ teaspoon white pepper, plus more

4 boneless skinless chicken breasts

2 tablespoons extra-virgin olive oil

4 tablespoons grapeseed or rapeseed oil

110g diced onion

180ml white wine

180ml chicken stock

130g mushrooms, sliced 0.5cm thick

150g seedless green grapes

Meat

Meat

In decorating, I love to mix the old and the new. That goes for my cooking approach too. 'Modern' meat dishes are a happy marriage of traditional, contemporary, and even trendy.

Take Rib Steak with Herb Dressing, which begins with a traditional American favourite – the steak – but gets a tenfold flavour boost from its tantalising herb dressing, spooned onto the cooked meat. This Italian technique is a mighty tool for kosher cooks, as versatile dressings are simple to make, require no ingredient hunting, and can be done beforehand. Lamb kofta, a traditional Turkish minced-meat bite, gets a distinctly modern-gourmet treatment with the addition of coriander, as does Stuffed Veal Breast with Chicken Livers and Prunes, the latter ingredients a classic combo that add last-word sophistication to a simple but savoury braise.

Kosher cooks should be alert to dishes like Braised Lamb Shanks, a time-honoured dish that's nonetheless made a restaurant comeback. A terrific braise that virtually cooks itself, the dish is perfect for food-loving diners, as is Savoury Thin Ribs, another homely dish that's been in vogue recently and that kosher cooks should add to their repertoire. I thought of calling the latter Modern Thin Ribs, as the ribs used are flanken-style, taken from the same part of the cow as the flanken Jewish cooks traditionally boil or use in soup. Now the cut is high quality fare.

Having said all this, there are certain culinary 'antiques' I honour because they're basic to Jewish cooking. Bubbie's Brisket is one, presented here just as my grandmother Goldie made it – she'd have killed me if I didn't! – and it's wonderful, juicy, tender, and deeply satisfying. Another venerable inclusion, but one with much more polish, is Standing Rib Roast. This supreme dinner party dish is really simple to do – fine cuts need little fussing with – and offers dining thrills, both visual and on the tongue. The moral, when it comes to kosher-dish making, is everything old can be new again – and should be.

Rib Steak with Herb Dressing

serves 4

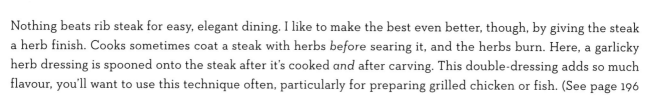

Nothing beats rib steak for easy, elegant dining. I like to make the best even better, though, by giving the steak a herb finish. Cooks sometimes coat a steak with herbs *before* searing it, and the herbs burn. Here, a garlicky herb dressing is spooned onto the steak after it's cooked *and* after carving. This double-dressing adds so much flavour, you'll want to use this technique often, particularly for preparing grilled chicken or fish. (See page 196 for an additional dressing recipe, but feel free to improvise your own.)

Geila's Tips

The easiest way to determine steak doneness is to press the meat with your finger as it cooks. If the meat feels very soft, like the flesh beneath your thumb, it's rare; if it feels medium-firm, like that same flesh after you've made a fist, it's medium; if it feels very firm, like the tip of your nose, it's well done.

Don't be tempted to buy boneless steaks. Meat cooked on the bone has superior flavour to that cooked with the bone removed.

Herb Dressing

120ml extra-virgin olive oil

5g fresh rosemary leaves

2 tablespoons flat-leaf parsley

4 garlic cloves

1½ teaspoons kosher salt

2 x 680g rib steaks, bone in,
at room temperature

1. To make the dressing, place all the ingredients in a small food processor (or use a hand blender and bowl). Purée, transfer to a small bowl and set aside.

2. Preheat a griddle pan or heavy frying pan large enough to accommodate the steaks over a high heat. Alternatively, preheat the grill or barbecue.

3. Dry the meat well with kitchen paper. Sauté the meat until brown on the bottom side, 4-5 minutes. Turn and sauté until cooked to desired doneness, starting to check after 5 minutes. Alternatively, cook under the grill or on a barbecue, turning once.

4. Transfer the steak to a chopping board and brush both sides with the dressing. Cover the steaks loosely with foil and allow to rest for 10 minutes.

5. Cut the steaks from the bones and slice the meat 1cm thick. Brush with the dressing and serve.

Bubbie's Brisket

serves 10–12

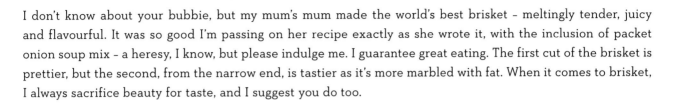

I don't know about your bubbie, but my mum's mum made the world's best brisket – meltingly tender, juicy and flavourful. It was so good I'm passing on her recipe exactly as she wrote it, with the inclusion of packet onion soup mix – a heresy, I know, but please indulge me. I guarantee great eating. The first cut of the brisket is prettier, but the second, from the narrow end, is tastier as it's more marbled with fat. When it comes to brisket, I always sacrifice beauty for taste, and I suggest you do too.

1. Preheat the oven to 150ºC/gas mark 2. Place the meat on a plate and rub both sides with the paprika, salt and pepper.

2. In a heavy frying pan or casserole dish, heat 2–3 tablespoons of the oil, depending on brisket size, over a medium-high heat. Add the brisket and sear on all sides without burning, about 12–15 minutes. Transfer to a plate. The brisket will be very dark.

3. Add more oil to the frying pan, if needed, then add the onions, carrots, celery and garlic, and sauté, stirring, until just beginning to soften and brown, 6–8 minutes. Transfer the vegetables to a roasting pan just large enough to hold the brisket, and top with the brisket.

4. In a large measuring jug, combine the wine, passata and soup mix. Add to the frying pan and deglaze over a medium-high heat, stirring, about 1 minute. Adjust the seasoning, if necessary. Pour the mixture over the brisket, adding more wine or water, if needed, so the liquid fills the pan by 1cm. Cover with foil and roast the brisket until tender, turning occasionally, and adding more wine or water, if necessary, about 5 hours. Leave the meat to cool in the pan and refrigerate overnight.

5. Remove the chilled fat from the meat and slice the meat 0.5cm thick, or as desired, and return to the pan. Heat, and serve with the sauce on the side.

Geila's Tip

If you like a thicker sauce, purée the cooked vegetables and return them to the pan before the brisket is reheated.

1 x 2–3kg brisket

2 tablespoons paprika

1 tablespoon kosher salt, plus more if needed

1 tablespoon freshly ground black pepper, plus more if needed

3 tablespoons grapeseed or rapeseed oil, plus more if needed

3–4 very large onions, cut into 1cm dice

6 medium carrots, peeled and sliced 1cm thick

6 celery stalks, sliced 1cm thick

5 garlic cloves

120ml red wine, plus more, if needed

240ml passata

1 x 50g packet French onion soup

Lamb Kofta

serves 4-6

Everyone needs a butcher like mine. A few years ago I asked him for a lamb rack, which arrived with 1kg of minced lamb gratis. What to do with my windfall? I remembered some delicious kofta - spicy meatballs - I'd enjoyed in Turkey, and headed to the kitchen. The result of my kofta experiment features pine nuts for texture and coriander for distinctive flavour. The tahini sauce provides a creamy accompaniment and can also be used as a dip. Serve the kofta with grilled vegetables, and you've got a great, informal meal.

1½ tablespoons extra-virgin olive oil

1½ tablespoons grapeseed or rapeseed oil, plus more for brushing

230g diced onion

3 garlic cloves, finely chopped

1 teaspoon kosher salt

32g pine nuts

900g minced lamb

12g breadcrumbs, made from fresh bread

2 tablespoons chopped coriander

2 teaspoons cumin

½ teaspoon freshly ground black pepper

Tahini Sauce (page 140), for serving

1. In a medium frying pan, heat the oils over a medium-high heat. Add the onion and garlic, season with ¼ teaspoon of the salt and sauté, stirring, until the onions are soft and beginning to brown, about 5-8 minutes. Transfer to a large bowl.

2. Add the pine nuts to the pan and toast over a medium heat, stirring, until they begin to colour and are aromatic, about 3 minutes. Watch carefully as they can burn easily. Transfer to the bowl.

3. Add the lamb, breadcrumbs, coriander, cumin, pepper and remaining salt, and combine lightly with your hands. Shape into patties about the size of a flattened golf ball, and transfer to a baking tray.

4. Heat a griddle pan or heavy frying pan over a medium-high heat, or preheat the grill or barbecue to high. Brush the kofta with oil. If using a griddle pan or frying pan, brush the pan with oil too. Fry or grill the kofta, turning once, to desired doneness, about 8 minutes for medium. The firmer the kofta to the touch, the greater the doneness. Transfer to plates and serve with the tahini sauce.

Braised Lamb Shanks

serves 4

'Modern' cooking is sometimes about cultural borrowing. Braised lamb shanks are a Middle Eastern speciality that bring sophistication to a kosher table. Richly flavoured, they make a terrific, hearty meal that's perfect for winter dining. They're also less expensive than their Italian cousin, osso buco, so you can serve them often, partnered with a creamy side dish like polenta and topped with a delicious tomato-rich sauce.

2 tablespoons grapeseed or rapeseed oil

4 lamb foreshanks, tied

2 tablespoons extra-virgin olive oil

6 garlic cloves, crushed with the side of a knife

2 celery sticks, cut into 1cm dice

2 large carrots, peeled and cut into 1cm dice

2 large onions, roughly chopped

4 tablespoons tomato purée

240ml dry white wine

480ml chicken stock

2 x 400g tins peeled plum tomatoes

1 bay leaf

2 sprigs fresh thyme

2 sprigs rosemary

8 peppercorns

1. Preheat the oven to 180ºC/gas mark 4. Heat the grapeseed oil in a large frying pan over a medium heat. Add the lamb and brown on all sides, 15-20 minutes. Set the shanks aside.

2. In the same pan, heat the olive oil, and the garlic, celery, carrots and onions, and sauté, scraping up any remaining meat bits, until soft, about 10 minutes. Push the vegetables to one side, add the tomato purée and cook until fragrant, about 4 minutes. Stir the vegetables into the paste, add the wine and bring to the boil. Boil for 2 minutes, add the stock, tomatoes, bay leaf, thyme, rosemary and peppercorns, and return to the boil.

3. Transfer the shanks to a roasting pan just large enough to hold them in a single layer, pour the braising liquid over the vegetables, cover with foil and bake for 1 hour. Uncover and turn the shanks over. Cook until the meat falls from the bone, about 2 hours, turning the shanks every 30 minutes. If the liquid gets too thick, add water.

4. Transfer the shanks to a plate. Strain the liquid into a measuring jug or fat separator and remove the fat. Remove the herbs and return them to the liquid. For a smooth sauce, purée the vegetables using a hand blender or ordinary blender. Serve the shanks with some of the sauce spooned over and the rest passed around in a sauce boat.

Standing Rib Roast
serves 12–16

A standing rib roast is royal dining – and a 'modern' building block that will help expand your kosher cooking repertoire. The key is to buy the best meat you can afford and do as little to it as possible. I like to stud the meat with garlic before it's roasted, but other than salt and pepper, that's about all the seasoning it gets. This is also an easy recipe to do: once the roast is in the oven, you can go about your business until it's time to check for doneness. And there's virtually no side dish that doesn't complement the roast, and vice versa.

To prepare the roast, the butcher removes the bones, replaces them, and then ties the roast to maintain its shape. When the roast is done, the bones are easily removed for carving. Save the bones, however; they're great to gnaw on.

Geila's Tip

This is a large roast, but feel free to buy a smaller one; just scale down the other ingredients proportionally.

1 x 7-bone beef rib (5–7kg), trimmed, bones removed and replaced, tied, at room temperature

12 garlic cloves, sliced 0.5cm thick

4–6 large onions, cut into eighths

4 tablespoons sea or kosher salt

56g cracked black pepper

1 bottle dry red wine

1. Preheat the oven to 220ºC/gas mark 7. With the point of a paring knife, make slits over the meat's surface and near the bones. Push the garlic into the slits.

2. Spread the onions in a large roasting pan and top with the meat, bone side down. Rub the meat with the salt and pepper, pour over the wine and roast until browned, about 20 minutes. Reduce the heat to 170ºC/gas mark 3 and cook to an internal temperature of 49–52ºC, or 12–14 minutes per 450g, for medium rare.

3. Transfer the meat to a chopping board, tent with foil, and leave to rest for 20 minutes. Remove the strings and bones, slice and serve with the onions.

Savoury Thin Ribs

serves 6

I always choose flanken thin ribs – cut through the bone so each piece consists of a thin meat strip with three or four oval slices of rib bone – as opposed to the single-bone kind. Here, the ribs get a wine braise, from which they emerge fall-off-the-bone tender and deliciously glazed. Served over a vegetable purée, the ribs are yet another cold-weather feast. Feel free to make this ahead of time, refrigerate and reheat; in fact, the ribs are even better the next day.

1. Preheat the oven to 180oC/gas mark 4. Dry the ribs well with kitchen paper and season with the pepper.

2. In a large ovenproof casserole, heat the oils over a medium-high heat. Working in batches if necessary, add the flanken and brown on the three meaty sides. Avoid crowding. Transfer the ribs to a plate and set aside.

3. Add the onion, shallots, carrots, celery and garlic to the pan and sauté, stirring, until browned, 6–8 minutes. Transfer the vegetables to the plate. Add the wine to the pan, deglaze, and reduce the liquid by half, about 10 minutes. Add the vinegar and sugar, and simmer to reduce the liquid by half, about 8 minutes. Return the meat to the pan, tuck the thyme around it, and add the stock.

4. Cover the pan, transfer to the oven, and cook for 2 hours. After the first hour, check to make sure the liquid fills the pan by 2.5cm; if not, add more stock. Return the vegetables to the pan, and cook until the meat barely stays on the bones, about 1 hour more.

5. If serving the same day, transfer the liquid to a large measuring jug or fat separator. Leave to stand for 30 minutes, skim the fat and return the liquid to the pan. If serving the following day, allow the ribs and liquid to come to room temperature, refrigerate, and skim the fat from the liquid. Simmer the liquid over a medium-high heat until syrupy, 10–15 minutes, periodically basting the meat with the liquid. Carefully transfer the ribs to plates, spoon the sauce over and serve.

6 flanken thin ribs (about 450g each)

2 tablespoons freshly ground black pepper

2 tablespoons extra-virgin olive oil

2 tablespoons grapeseed or rapeseed oil

1 large onion, cut into 0.5cm dice

12 shallots, halved

2 carrots, peeled and cut into 0.5cm dice

2 celery stalks, cut into 0.5cm dice

3 garlic cloves, finely chopped

1 bottle dry fruity red wine

2 tablespoons balsamic vinegar

2 tablespoons sugar

4 thyme sprigs

950ml veal stock (page 192) or chicken stock, plus more if needed

Stuffed Veal Breast with Chicken Livers and Prunes

serves 6

I love to braise; the technique produces deeply delicious food that needs little attention while cooking. Veal breast makes a meltingly tender braise that's unexpectedly sophisticated when stuffed with chicken livers and prunes – a classic combo that I've reworked so neither overpowers the other. Ask your butcher to make the pocket for stuffing – and serve this to food-loving friends who don't mind picking for the most savoury parts.

1. First make the stuffing. In a small bowl, combine the porcini with 240ml of boiling water and soak until soft, about 20 minutes. Strain and chop the porcini. Set aside with the water.

2. In a medium frying pan, heat the oil over a medium heat. Add the shallots and sauté, until translucent. Add the livers, prunes, porcini, salt, pepper and sage, and sauté until fragrant, 2–3 minutes. Add the port, avert your face, and ignite with a barbecue lighter or match. Cook until almost all of the liquid has evaporated. Remove half of the prunes and set aside.

3. Transfer the stuffing mixture to a food processor. Combine with the breadcrumbs and eggs, and pulse until smooth. Transfer the stuffing to a medium bowl, add the remaining prunes and blend. Set aside.

4. Preheat the oven to 180ºC/gas mark 4. Heat 2 tablespoons of the oil in a roasting pan and heat until hot but not smoking. Add the celery, carrots, onion, thyme, bay leaf and peppercorns, and sauté, stirring, until soft but not brown, 8–10 minutes. Add the garlic and sauté for 2 minutes. Sprinkle with the flour and sauté, stirring, 2 minutes. Add the wine and reduce by half. Add the reserved porcini liquid and simmer to blend the flavours, about 5 minutes. Transfer to a medium bowl and set aside.

5. Open the veal pocket, stuff with the liver mixture and secure the open side with kitchen twine. Season the veal on all sides with salt.

6. Return the roasting pan to the hob and heat the remaining oil over a medium heat. Place the veal in the pan, and brown well, turning once, 15–20 minutes. Reduce the heat if the veal begins to burn. Position the veal bone side down and add the reserved vegetable mixture and stock. Bring to the boil, cover the pan tightly with foil, and bake until a bone can be easily pulled from the roast, 2½–3 hours. Transfer the roast to a chopping board, tent with foil and leave to rest for 20 minutes.

7. Meanwhile, strain the pan contents through a fine-mesh sieve into a large measuring jug, pressing down the solids. Discard the fat. For a chunky sauce, discard the herbs and return the vegetables to the sauce.

8. Remove the bones from the veal, carve and serve with the sauce.

Stuffing

15g dried porcini

2 tablespoons grapeseed or rapeseed oil

3 shallots, finely chopped

225g chicken livers (see page 18 for kashering)

225g prunes, chopped

1 teaspoon salt

½ teaspoon white pepper

3 tablespoons finely chopped fresh sage, or 1 tablespoon dried

60ml port

80g breadcrumbs

2 medium eggs

6 tablespoons grapeseed or rapeseed oil

2 celery stalks, finely chopped

2 carrots, peeled, finely chopped

1 large onion, finely chopped

3 sprigs thyme

1 bay leaf

8 black peppercorns

5 garlic cloves, crushed with the side of a knife

3 tablespoons plain flour

360ml white wine

1 x 2–3kg veal breast, bone in, with pocket

kosher salt

950ml veal or beef stock (page 192), or chicken stock

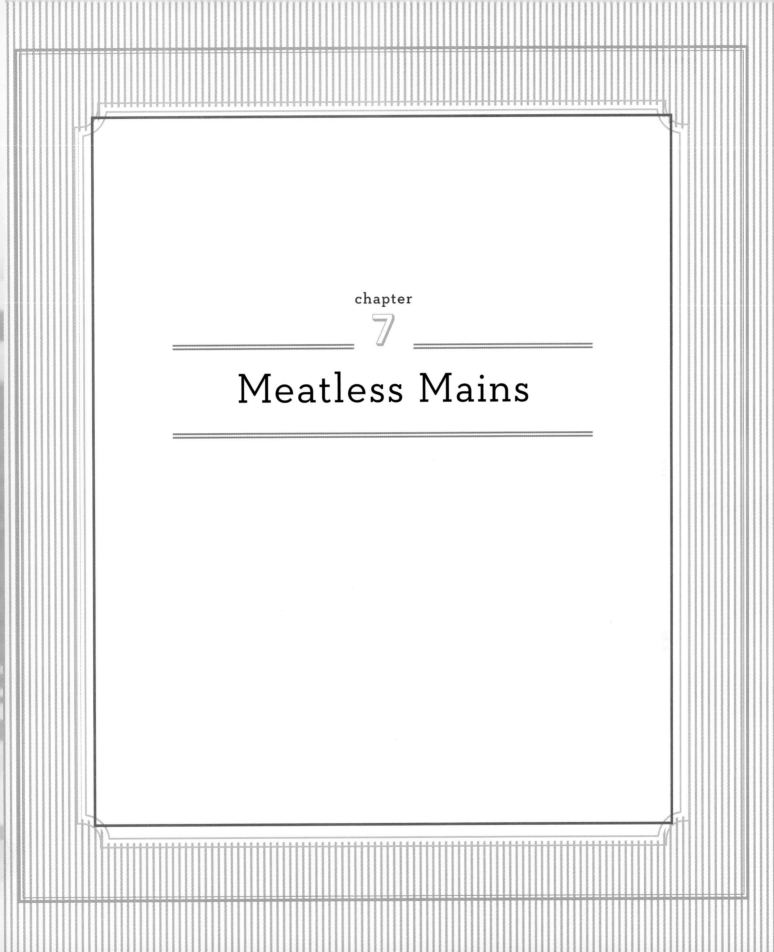

chapter

7

Meatless Mains

Meatless Mains

I love meat, but these days I'm apt to crave dishes without it. Other cultures boast large repertoires of delicious meatless mains, and it's time we caught up with them. For the kosher cook, non-meat dishes are especially versatile.

Take Cauliflower Paneer Masala. It's based on spicy Indian masala dishes, but features paneer, a soothing fresh cheese you make yourself. Substitute tofu for the paneer, and the dish is pareve. Cold Sesame Noodles with Broccoli and Tofu also features that Asian speciality, fried for tempting texture. Like so many other 'modern' dishes, it owes its existence to our expanded kosher store cupboard. Thank that store cupboard as well for Tess's Penne with Blue Cheese, Pecans and Sultanas, a terrifically appealing dish my daughter devised when kosher blue cheese became available.

I'm particularly pleased with the Linguine with Roasted Tomatoes and Courgettes, a pareve dish with a Parmesan-like topping. That cheeseless finish is provided by 'pareve Parmesan', a breadcrumb, pine nut and sea salt mixture I devised that has the richness and texture of actual Parmesan. I store the blend and use it for casseroles and other dishes, and I think you'll want to as well.

Everyone loves a good risotto, and Risotto Primavera, a creamy blend of rice and fresh vegetables, is a star among those satisfying dishes. Most risottos are 'meat' because they're made with chicken or beef stock, but this is dairy, as vegetable stock is used instead. It's an example of finding (or devising) a non-meat version of dishes that typically include it – creative thinking that's basic to the 'modern' approach.

Aubergine Rollatini – aubergine slices that enclose a meatless filling – is familiar to many kosher cooks. In my version the sauce includes smoky roasted red peppers, a distinctly modern touch that elevates a too-often humdrum dish. Asparagus and Mushroom lasagne, another kosher warhorse, is also given vibrant life through attentive vegetable cooking, the inclusion of sun-dried tomatoes and the substitution of béchamel for the usual mozzarella, which can become stringy.

Did I say these dishes are versatile? They're meant to be mains, but they also work beautifully as sides. It's funny. Kosher keepers often eat 'meatless' outside the house, without considering that they can enjoy even better non-meat dishes at home. Now they can.

Cold Sesame Noodles with Broccoli and Tofu

serves 4

Everyone loves cold sesame noodles, an addictively delicious meal-in-one that also keeps well. Here's my version, which features fried tofu for textural contrast. This is another dish that kosher cooks couldn't make until chilli oil and rice wine vinegar became part of the kosher store cupboard. I serve this a lot in summer – and the rest of the year too.

Convert It

To make this a meat dish, add diced grilled or poached chicken in place of the tofu and substitute chicken stock for the water.

Sauce

4 tablspoons tahini (sesame paste)

75g smooth peanut butter

2 tablespoons soy sauce

1 tablespoon rice wine vinegar

1 teaspoon grated ginger

⅛–¼ teaspoon chilli oil, to taste

2 tablespoons sugar

400g firm tofu

113g fresh broccoli florets, or frozen and defrosted under hot tap water

3 tablespoons grapeseed or rapeseed oil

340g linguine

2 tablespoons sesame seeds, for garnish

1. In a 500ml measuring jug or hand blender beaker, combine the sauce ingredients and 3 tablespoons of water and, using a hand blender, blend until smooth. Alternatively, use a regular blender. Transfer to a large bowl.

2. Place a clean tea towel on a work surface. Place the tofu on top of the towel and fold the towel to enclose it. Top the tofu with a plate and add a weight, such as a heavy tin. Allow the tofu to drain for 30 minutes. Cut the tofu into 2.5cm dice and set aside.

3. If using fresh broccoli, bring abundant salted water to the boil. Add the broccoli and blanch until deeply coloured and slightly softened, about 4 minutes. Remove the broccoli with a large sieve and run under cold tap water. Drain and transfer to the large bowl.

4. In a large frying pan, heat the oil over a medium-high heat. Add the tofu and sauté, stirring, until golden, about 4 minutes. Transfer the tofu to kitchen paper to drain. Set aside.

5. Bring fresh abundant salted water to the boil in a large pan. Add the linguine, and cook until al dente, following the packet instructions. Drain the pasta, transfer to the bowl with the broccoli and sauce, and toss. Add the tofu, toss and leave to cool to room temperature before serving.

Risotto Primavera

serves 4

In the Seventies, pasta primavera was a dish you found everywhere. I first discovered it at Manhattan's Le Cirque restaurant, where it was invented, and made it as soon as the recipe was published, it was that good. Flash-forward to my present wish to create a risotto version. This is it – a wonderful combination of creamy rice and fresh vegetables that everyone loves, even kids. This recipe has a good number of ingredients, but once you've done your prep, everything goes together easily.

1. Fill a large frying pan two-thirds full with water and bring to the boil. Add the asparagus, string beans and courgettes, and blanch for 3 minutes. Drain, cool under cold tap water, drain and transfer to a medium bowl. Set aside.

2. In the same frying pan, heat 1 tablespoon each of the butter and oil over a medium-high heat. Add the mushrooms, sprinkle with salt, then add the thyme. Sauté, stirring, until the mushroom liquid has evaporated, about 4 minutes. Transfer to the bowl.

3. Wipe out the pan and add 1 tablespoon each of the butter and oil. Add the tomatoes, 1 garlic clove and the basil, and sprinkle with salt. Sauté over a medium-high heat, stirring gently, until the tomatoes have just softened, about 4 minutes. The tomatoes should retain their shape. Transfer to the bowl.

4. Wipe out the pan again, and add the remaining butter and oil. Add the remaining garlic clove, onion and carrot, and sauté over a medium-high heat, stirring, until the onion is translucent and the carrot is beginning to soften, 3-4 minutes. Add the rice and sauté, stirring constantly, until translucent except for a white dot at the centre, 1-2 minutes. Add the wine and cook, stirring gently, until the liquid has evaporated, 1-2 minutes.

5. Reduce the heat to medium-low and add the stock 120ml at a time until each is absorbed, stirring occasionally. Simmer until the rice is al dente, about 35 minutes. If the rice is too firm, add 120ml of boiling water and continue to cook.

6. Add the cream and stir to blend. Add the Parmesan and stir. Add the vegetables and peas, and mix well. If the rice seems sticky, add more boiling water to smooth it to a creamy consistency. Transfer to plates and serve.

Geila's Tip

Making risotto isn't hard, but it requires attention. Keep your eye on the rice as it simmers, never letting it to stick to the pan. Make sure the rice is cooked al dente - with a bit of bite at the centre.

50g peeled asparagus, cut into 0.5cm dice

70g green beans, cut into 0.5cm dice

140g courgettes, cut into 0.5cm dice

3 tablespoons unsalted butter

3 tablespoons grapeseed or rapeseed oil

30g mushrooms, cut into 0.5cm dice

kosher salt

2 thyme sprigs

2 large tomatoes, skinned, deseeded and diced

2 garlic cloves, finely chopped

10 basil leaves, julienned

55g finely chopped onion

1 carrot, peeled and cut into 0.5cm dice

190g Arborio rice

120ml dry white wine

700ml vegetable stock (page 193), heated

3 tablespoons double cream

75-80g grated Parmesan

60g frozen peas, defrosted under hot tap water, drained

Cauliflower Paneer Masala

serves 6

Asian cooking is a kosher cook's best friend. With large vegetable-dish repertoires, it offers unlimited good eating to those who want to eat meatless and well. Take this richly spiced cauliflower paneer, a traditional Indian favourite. For years I searched for kosher paneer - a compressed cottage-cheese-like ingredient that adds soothing milkiness to otherwise hot dishes - then realised it was simple to make my own. Served over rice, this is a great meal in itself that goes together quickly once you've got the ingredients on hand.

Convert It

To make this dish pareve, omit the butter, double the quantity of oil, and use cubed tofu in place of the paneer.

Masala

1–2 jalapeño peppers, to taste

3 garlic cloves

2.5cm ginger, peeled

2 tablespoons unsalted butter

5 tablespoons grapeseed or rapeseed oil

1 teaspoon ground cumin

1 teaspoon coriander seed

2 medium onions, roughly chopped

2 x 400g tins peeled tomatoes, chopped, with juice, if needed

3 tablespoons grapeseed or rapeseed oil

1 head cauliflower, cut into florets, or 340g frozen cauliflower florets, defrosted

1 teaspoon kosher salt

½ teaspoon turmeric

¼ teaspoon cayenne, or to taste

1 tablespoon garam masala

1½ teaspoons powdered coriander

225g paneer (page 194), cut into 2.5cm cubes

cooked rice, for serving

20g chopped coriander, for garnish

1. First make the masala. In a mini food processor, combine the jalapeño, garlic and ginger, and pulse until finely chopped. Alternatively, chop by hand. Heat a large frying pan over a medium-high heat. Add the butter and oil, and when very hot but not smoking, add the cumin and coriander seed. Add the onions and tomatoes without juice and simmer until thickened, about 10 minutes. Purée using a hand blender or an ordinary blender, and set aside.

2. Add 1 tablespoon of the oil to the pan and heat over a medium heat. Add the cauliflower, salt, turmeric, cayenne, garam masala, powdered coriander, and toss. Add the reserved masala mixture, partially cover, and simmer until the cauliflower is tender, 15–30 minutes. If the mixture seems dry, add some of the reserved tomato juice.

3. Meanwhile, in a small frying pan, heat the remaining oil over a medium-high heat. Add the paneer and sauté, stirring, until golden, 2–3 minutes. Transfer to kitchen paper to drain.

4. When the cauliflower is almost cooked, add the paneer to the pan, toss, and simmer to blend the flavours, about 10 minutes. If the mixture seems dry, add the reserved tomato juice, or water if none is left.

5. Divide the rice among serving plates. Garnish with the coriander and serve.

Tess's Penne with Blue Cheese, Pecans and Sultanas

serves 6

At nine years old, my daughter Tess said to me one day, 'Mum, you look tired. I'm going to cook my dinner.' And 45 minutes and a thousand used pans later she asked me to taste this dish, which was terrific. Truly, I thought, the apple doesn't fall far from the – well, you know. While I've made some modifications, the dish remains hers – penne with crunchy pecans in a creamy blue-cheese sauce, whose saltiness is balanced by the sweet sultanas.

1. Bring an abundant quantity of water to the boil. Add the salt and pasta, and cook until almost al dente, following the packet instructions. Drain. Reserve 240ml of the cooking water.

2. Meanwhile, heat the butter and oil in a large frying pan over a medium-high heat. Add the shallots, thyme and garlic, and cook until the shallots are translucent, 2–3 minutes. Add the cream and Gorgonzola, stir until the cheese is melted, reduce the heat and barely simmer until the mixture begins to thicken, 4–6 minutes. Add the sultanas.

3. Remove the thyme and fresh garlic cloves, if used. Transfer the pasta to the pan, add the Parmesan and pecans and about 120ml of the reserved pasta water. Increase the heat and simmer until the sauce is shiny and thickened and coats the pasta. Season lightly with pepper, toss and serve.

2 tablespoons kosher salt

450g penne

1 tablespoon unsalted butter

1 tablespoon walnut, grapeseed or rapeseed oil

2 shallots, finely chopped

2 thyme sprigs

2 roasted garlic cloves, or 1 clove, crushed with the side of a knife

225ml double cream

115g Gorgonzola, or 85g other blue cheese

45g sultanas

40g grated Parmesan

50g chopped pecans

freshly ground black pepper

Aubergine Rollatini
serves 6

Baked aubergine slices rolled around a meatless filling is a well-loved kosher dish. My version ups the traditional ante as it's served with a sauce that includes smoky red peppers, a great aubergine counterpoint, plus creamy mascarpone. The dish is luscious but light, and can also be made in advance (see Tip). It's a great family favourite.

1. Place the aubergine slices on kitchen paper and sprinkle on both sides with the 2 tablespoons of salt. Allow the slices to release their bitter juices, 20-30 minutes.

2. To make the sauce, cut the tomatoes in large chunks, combine with the peppers in a medium bowl and purée with a hand blender, or in a food processor. Heat a large frying pan over a medium-high heat. Add the tomato and pepper purée, basil, garlic, oregano and 1 teaspoon of the salt, bring to the boil, reduce the heat and simmer until the flavours are blended, 15-20 minutes. Set aside.

3. Meanwhile, preheat the oven to 180°C/gas mark 4. Cover 2 medium baking trays with foil and brush with the olive oil.

4. Wipe the excess salt from the aubergine slices, roll in the kitchen paper and squeeze the rolls gently to remove more moisture. Transfer the slices to the baking trays, and bake until tender and somewhat translucent, 15-20 minutes. Cover the slices with foil (to trap steam that will prevent the aubergine from sticking to the pan) and allow to cool.

5. Meanwhile, in a large bowl, combine the ricotta, mascarpone, nutmeg and the remaining teaspoon of salt. Transfer half of the tomato sauce to a large baking dish.

6. Using 2-3 tablespoons of the cheese mixture, shape it into balls. Place a ball at one end of an aubergine slice, roll to enclose it, and transfer to the baking dish, seam side down. Repeat with the remaining cheese mixture and aubergine slices. Spoon the remaining tomato sauce over the aubergine, sprinkle with the Parmesan and bake until tender, about 20 minutes. Leave to rest for 5-10 minutes before serving.

Geila's Tip

You can prepare the filling or sauce beforehand and refrigerate. Or bake the dish, allow it to cool, and refrigerate. Bring it to room temperature and serve.

---

3 medium aubergines, sliced lengthways 1cm thick (about 18 slices)

2 tablespoons plus 2 teaspoons kosher salt

2 x 400g tins peeled plum tomatoes

2 roasted red peppers (see Step 3, page 48)

2 large basil sprigs

6 puréed roasted garlic cloves

2 sprigs fresh oregano, or 2 teaspoons dried

60ml extra-virgin olive oil

425g ricotta

100g mascarpone

⅛-¼ teaspoon freshly grated nutmeg, to taste

40g grated Parmesan

Linguine with Roasted Tomatoes and Courgettes

serves 4

This savoury pasta dish began with a surplus of tomatoes and courgettes – and the wish to make a pareve dish that had a Parmesan-like finish *without* cheese. The result was the creation of 'pareve Parmesan', a breadcrumb and pine nut mixture I'm really excited about. The crumbs and nuts provide texture; cheese-like richness is supplied by the sauce, which contains anchovies with their oil. But anchovy-phobes will be happy, as the dish has zero anchovy flavour. I hope you'll devise other ways to use pareve Parmesan, one of my store-cupboard basics (see Tip), and serve this luscious dish often.

Convert It

To make this dairy, use 100g of grated Parmesan in place of the breadcrumb and pine nut mixture.

Geila's Tip

You can make the 'pareve Parmesan' – the breadcrumb, salt and pine nut mixture – in advance. Store it in an air-tight container in the fridge for up to 3 weeks.

Pareve Parmesan

40g breadcrumbs

1 teaspoon grapeseed or rapeseed oil

65g pine nuts

2 teaspoons sea salt or kosher salt

450g cherry tomatoes, halved

6 tablespoons extra-virgin olive oil

1 tablespoon sugar

1 tablespoon balsamic vinegar

3 medium shallots, finely sliced

680g courgettes, cut into 0.5cm dice

1 tablespoon plus 3 teaspoons kosher salt

340g linguini

1 x 50g tin anchovies with the oil

⅛ teaspoon chilli flakes

1½ tablespoons chopped fresh oregano, or 1 teaspoon dried

1. First make the pareve Parmesan. Preheat the oven to 170°C/gas mark 3. Spread the breadcrumbs on a baking sheet, bake until golden, about 5 minutes, and transfer to a mini food processor or blender. Meanwhile, heat the oil in a small frying pan over a medium heat. Add the nuts and toast, stirring, until fragrant, about 4 minutes. Transfer to the processor and pulse to chop. Transfer the mixture to a small bowl, add the salt and stir well. Set aside.

2. Increase the oven temperature to 190°C/gas mark 5. Place the tomatoes in a small roasting pan, add 2 tablespoons of the olive oil, sugar, vinegar, shallots and 1 teaspoon of the kosher salt, and toss. Arrange the tomatoes in a single layer and set aside.

3. Line a baking tray with foil. Place the courgettes on the sheet and toss with 2 teaspoons of the kosher salt and 2 tablespoons of the oil. Place the tomatoes and the courgettes in the oven. Bake the courgettes until tender and beginning to brown, 20–30 minutes. Bake the tomatoes, stirring occasionally and rearranging them in a single layer as necessary, until shrivelled and their juice has almost evaporated, about 45 minutes. Set the courgettes and tomatoes aside.

4. Bring a large pan of water to the boil and add the remaining kosher salt. Add the linguine and cook until al dente, following packet instructions. Reserve 480ml of the cooking water. Meanwhile, in a mini food processor or blender, combine the anchovies with their oil, chilli flakes, oregano and the remaining 2 tablespoons of olive oil, and purée.

5. Heat a large frying pan over a medium-high heat. Add the tomatoes, courgettes, anchovy mixture and pasta, and toss. Add 120ml of the reserved cooking water and simmer to thicken the sauce, 1–2 minutes. Add more water by 120ml measures, if necessary, to smooth out the sauce. Remove the pasta from the heat, add the pareve Parmesan and toss. Transfer to plates and serve.

Asparagus and Mushroom Lasagne

serves 8

I've had my share of vegetable lasagnes and most were less than great. Then I enjoyed a marvellous version at an Italian restaurant. The vegetables were fresh tasting, there was no stringy mozzarella, and the fusion of pasta and béchamel was just right. I wanted more. Here's my version of that dish – vivid tasting and completely satisfying. Feel free to make this with other veggies of your choice, such as artichoke hearts or cubed baked butternut squash. Just be sure to rid them of all excess vegetable liquid before you assemble the lasagne.

Geila's Tip

You can use fresh or dried lasagne sheets for this.

1 tablespoon grapeseed or rapeseed oil

3 tablespoons unsalted butter, at room temperature

225g mushrooms, finely sliced

pinch of kosher salt

60ml white wine

340g asparagus, peeled if medium-large, trimmed, cut on the diagonal into 1cm lengths

225g lasagne sheets, fresh or dried

700ml béchamel (page 196), made with milk only

120g grated Parmesan, or more, if desired

1 x 170g jar sun-dried tomato paste, drained of excess oil

1. In a small frying pan, heat the oil and 1 tablespoon of butter over a medium-high heat. Add the mushrooms, sprinkle with salt, and sauté until soft and all liquid has been absorbed, about 4 minutes. Add the wine and cook until it has been absorbed, about 2 minutes. Set aside.

2. Preheat the oven to 180ºC/gas mark 4. Bring a large pan of salted water to the boil. Add the asparagus and cook until tender, about 3 minutes. Remove the asparagus with a sieve, run under cold water to stop the cooking and set aside. Return the water to the boil, add the lasagne, and cook until al dente, 2 minutes if fresh, or follow packet instructions if dry. Drain the lasagne, run under cold water and transfer to a clean tea towel to dry.

3. Spray a large baking dish that can be brought to the table with non-stick cooking spray. Add 120ml of béchamel and spread to coat the bottom of the pan. Add a layer of lasagne, 120ml of béchamel, ⅓ of the mushrooms, ⅓ of the asparagus, 25g of Parmesan and ⅓ of the tomato paste. Repeat 2 more times, ending with a layer of lasagne. Spread the remaining béchamel on top and sprinkle with the remaining Parmesan, or more if desired. Dot with the remaining 2 tablespoons of butter and bake until bubbling and golden, 15-20 minutes. Leave to rest for at least 15 minutes, cut and serve.

chapter

8

Sides

Sides

You'd expect 'modern' sides to be versatile, and they are. Most are pareve or are easily converted.

Baby Pak Choi with Garlic, for example, can be made in pareve, meat and dairy versions, and each reveals a deliciously different take on this versatile braise. Broccoli Soufflé, a golden-topped pudding that I call neo-kugel, can be pareve, dairy or meat, as can Glazed Brussels Sprouts with Chestnuts. So can Sweetcorn with Sage Flan, a silky side that's a perfect mate to any non-saucy fish or meat main. I'm a great lover of savoury flans, so I also offer a Velvet Parmesan version, a lusciously cheesy side that's a bit fancy but also easily done.

Central to the adaptability of many of the sides is my pareve béchamel (also offered in a traditional dairy version), see page 196. Credit nut milk for the non-dairy creaminess of the pareve béchamel and for the sides, like Creamed Spinach, that include it. In my parents' day you'd have to make that dish with velouté sauce – chicken stock thickened with roux – to get the right texture. No more.

Some sides also work beautifully as mains. Middle Eastern Courgette Cakes with Tahini Sauce, a favourite at my table, is main course material for sure, as is Ratatouille Hash when prepared, as suggested, with chickpeas and crumbled feta, or with minced, sautéd lamb. Sweetcorn Salad, a toss of that sweet vegetable with peppers, onions and sesame oil-based dressing, can satisfy a hungry gathering with added tuna, grilled chicken or leftover steak.

Simple is usually best, and quickly made sides like Oven-Roasted New Potatoes and Glazed Shallots prove the point. The potatoes get a rosemary finish, but you can vary the herb to taste. To become golden and caramelised, glazed shallots once required a long time in the oven, but by following my method, you get the same result in much less time. Parsnip Purée is an equally quick-to-fix pareve dish that works with a wide range of mains, and trumps the usual mashed potatoes in flavour and healthfulness.

Delicious and adaptable, these and the other sides maximise your options while assuring great eating.

Ratatouille Hash

serves 10-12

I was in a restaurant on the beautiful Caribbean island, St Martin, when a waiter presented the table with ratatouille served in timbales. It was delicious – and set me to thinking about adapting the usual ratatouille, a vegetable stew, to make it less stewy. Here's the result, a vibrant, fragrant hash – every vegetable retains its distinctive texture as well as flavour – that makes a perfect meal served with chicken, fish or meat. You can serve it hot or at room temperature.

Convert It

To make this a dairy main course, add 115g tinned chickpeas, drained and rinsed, and crumbled feta. Or, for or a quick, moussaka-like dish, toss the hash with minced, sautéd lamb.

Geila's Tips

Check the bottom of the aubergines you buy. If the indentation is round, the plant is female; if long, male (which. have fewer seeds and are therefore less bitter.

2-3 medium aubergines, cut into 1cm cubes

4 tablespoons kosher salt, plus more

6 tablespoons extra-virgin olive oil

900g courgettes, cut into 1cm cubes

2 tablespoons grapeseed or rapeseed oil

2 large onions, finely sliced

2 tablespoons tomato purée

4 garlic cloves, put through a garlic press

2 roasted red peppers (see Step 3, page 48), cut into 0.5cm dice

2 tablespoons balsamic vinegar

1 tablespoon sugar

¼ teaspoon chilli flakes (optional)

170g tinned plum tomatoes with their juice

3 tablespoons chopped basil

1. Preheat the oven to 190ºC/gas mark 5. Cover 2 medium baking trays with foil.

2. Place the aubergine cubes in a colander in the sink and toss with 2 tablespoons of salt. Top with a plate and a weight, such as a large tin or wine bottle. Let the aubergines drain for 30 minutes, rinse and dry them, and transfer to a baking tray. Drizzle over 3 tablespoons of olive oil.

3. Place the courgette cubes on the second baking tray, toss with 2 tablespoons of salt and 3 tablespoons of olive oil. Bake the courgettes and the aubergines until cooked through, about 20 minutes, stirring both after 10 minutes to prevent sticking. Set both aside.

4. In a large frying pan, heat the grapeseed oil over a medium-high heat. Add the onions, sprinkle with salt and sauté, stirring, until translucent, 8-10 minutes. Push the onions to the side of the pan, add the tomato purée to the centre, and cook until the purée begins to bubble, about 4 minutes. Add the garlic and sauté the mixture until the garlic is fragrant, about 1 minute. Add the peppers, stir, then add the vinegar, sugar, chilli flakes, if using, and tomatoes with half of the juice, and simmer until most of the liquid has evaporated, about 4 minutes. Add the aubergines, courgettes and basil, reduce the heat to medium-low and simmer, stirring often, until the flavours have blended, about 10 minutes. If the mixture seems too dry, add more of the tomato juice and simmer for 4-5 minutes more. Adjust the seasoning, if necessary, transfer to plates and serve.

Broccoli Soufflé

serves 4-6

I call this delicious side neo-kugel, that pudding-like casserole usually made with noodles. It has something of kugel's appealing texture, but it's lighter. I make this with broccoli, but you can use cauliflower too. This is a very versatile vegetable dish that goes beautifully with just about any main course, meat, fish or poultry.

Convert It

To make this pareve, substitute pareve béchamel (page 196) for the dairy version and use vegetable stock (page 193) in place of the chicken stock. To make this a dairy dish, substitute milk for the stock and add 90g grated Cheddar cheese to the béchamel.

1 head broccoli, cut into florets

3 medium eggs, separated

60ml chicken stock

20g breadcrumbs

240ml pareve béchamel (page 196)

kosher salt

1. Preheat the oven to 170ºC/gas mark 3. Spray a 10 x 20.5cm soufflé dish with non-stick cooking spray.

2. Bring a large pan of abundant salted water to the boil. Add the broccoli and blanch until brightly coloured and slightly softened, about 4 minutes. Drain, cool under cold tap water, drain and dry.

3. In a medium bowl, combine the egg yolks with the chicken stock, and beat until beginning to thicken. Add the broccoli, breadcrumbs and béchamel, and mix well.

4. In a separate bowl, beat the egg whites with the salt until stiff but not dry. Fold the whites into the broccoli mixture and transfer to the soufflé dish. Bake until risen and golden, and a knife inserted into the soufflé comes out clean, 35-40 minutes. Allow to rest for 20 minutes. Unmould onto a large plate, or cut into serving pieces. Serve.

Creamed Spinach

serves 4-6

Creamed spinach is an old favourite that everyone enjoys. This pareve version, while deliciously creamy, avoids the excess richness of other versions so you can really taste the spinach. It's a natural accompaniment to a meat meal, though it's equally good with poached fish, or by itself, topped with a poached egg.

1. If using fresh spinach, wash the leaves and, without drying them, transfer to a large frying pan. Cook over a medium-high heat until wilted, 1-1½ minutes. Chop, squeeze to remove excess moisture, and set aside.

2. In a small frying pan, heat the oil over a medium heat, add the onion, sprinkle with salt and sauté, stirring, until the onions are translucent, about 5 minutes. Transfer to a medium bowl, add the spinach and béchamel, and stir to blend. Season with additional salt and pepper, and add the nutmeg if desired. Transfer to a warmed serving bowl and serve.

Convert It

To make this dairy, prepare the béchamel with butter instead of margarine (see page 196).

Geila's Tip

This may be made a day ahead. Allow the spinach to cool, place cling film directly on its surface and refrigerate. Reheat in the microwave for 1-2 minutes, stirring every 30 seconds, or in a saucepan, stirring frequently, over a low heat.

900g baby spinach leaves or 570g frozen chopped spinach

1 tablespoon grapeseed or rapeseed oil

1 small onion, cut into 0.5cm dice

kosher salt

360ml pareve béchamel (page 196), made with 3 tablespoons margarine, 4 tablespoons flour and 360ml soya milk

freshly ground black pepper

pinch nutmeg (optional)

Baby Pak Choi with Garlic

serves 4-6

I like to braise thicker vegetables like pak choi rather than sautéing or stir-frying them. You get all the fresh taste those methods can provide, but less oiliness – and the braising liquid adds another flavour layer. I serve this with my Miso-Glazed Cod (page 74) and anything, really, with which a garlicky green vegetable would go.

Convert It

To make this a meat dish, use chicken stock in place of the vegetable stock. To make this dairy, use butter in place of the olive oil.

2 tablespoons extra-virgin olive oil

2 tablespoons grapeseed or rapeseed oil

6 medium garlic cloves, finely chopped

8–10 (depending on number of servings) baby pak choi, well rinsed, halved

1½ teaspoons salt, plus more, if needed

2 x 30g packets G. Washington's Golden Seasoning and Broth (page 18), dissolved in 480ml water, or 480ml vegetable stock (page 193)

1. In a large frying pan, heat the oils over a medium-high heat. Add the garlic and sauté, stirring, until fragrant, 45-60 seconds. Don't allow the garlic to brown.

2. Add the pak choi and toss until coated with the oil. Sprinkle with the salt, add the stock and simmer until the pak choi is tender, 8-10 minutes. Adjust the seasoning, drain and serve.

Sweetcorn Salad

serves 6

This delicious - and beautiful - salad began with a bag of sweetcorn kernels I'd scraped from cobs served at a barbecue. In my house, company is a constant. To feed a hungry crowd one day and to use up the kernels, I invented this salad. With toasted pine nuts, onion, pepper and a tantalising sesame oil-based dressing, the salad goes beautifully with my Surimi Crab Cakes with Red Pepper Mayonnaise (page 72) or with any grilled meat or fish.

1. In a small frying pan, heat the oil over a medium heat. Add the nuts and toast, stirring, until aromatic and beginning to colour, about 3 minutes. Set the nuts aside.

2. Fill a large pan with water and bring to the boil. Taste the sweetcorn; if it's not sufficiently sweet, add the sugar to the water. Add the corn on the cobs and cook until just tender, 5-7 minutes. Drain, and when the cobs are cool, cut off the kernels using a large knife. Transfer the kernels to a large bowl.

3. Add the pepper, onion, spring onions, coriander and reserved nuts, and toss. In a small bowl, combine the sesame oil, vinegar, mirin and salt, and blend well. Pour over the sweetcorn mixture and toss well. Serve at room temperature or chilled.

Geila's Tip

Never add salt to the water in which you boil sweetcorn. It toughens the kernels.

1 teaspoon grapeseed or rapeseed oil

65g pine nuts

6 corn on the cobs

100g sugar, if needed

1 orange, yellow or red pepper, cored, deseeded and cut into 0.5cm dice

1 red onion, diced

4 spring onions, white part only, sliced

20g chopped coriander

1 tablespoon toasted sesame oil

1 tablespoon rice wine vinegar

1 tablespoon mirin

½ teaspoon kosher salt

Glazed Brussels Sprouts with Chestnuts

serves 6

I'm a great fan of chestnuts, which pair perfectly with Brussels sprouts. Now that kosher peeled chestnuts are available, making this perfect autumn side dish is a cinch. I prefer 'baby' Brussels sprouts, which are about a centimetre in diameter. Available around late November, they're sweeter than the larger kind. If you use them, chop the chestnuts smaller than directed. If you can't find baby Brussels sprouts, use the fully grown kind.

1. To prepare the sprouts, remove the outer leaves, rinse them and trim the stem ends. If using larger sprouts, cut an x in the stem ends.

2. Bring a large pan of salted water to the boil. Add the sprouts and cook until tender, 2-5 minutes, depending on size. Drain and rinse under cold water. Halve or quarter the sprouts, depending on size.

3. In a large frying pan, heat the oil over a medium-high heat. Add the shallots, sprinkle with salt, and sauté, stirring, until translucent, 2-3 minutes. Add the sprouts and wine, and simmer until the wine has evaporated, about 1 minute. Add the chestnuts and warm through. Test the sprouts for doneness; if not done, add a little water and continue to cook.

4. Add the mustard and turkey fat, and toss to coat the sprouts. Season with salt and serve.

Covert It

To make this pareve, use olive oil instead of the fat. For dairy, use butter.

Geila's Tip

The sprouts can be blanched a day ahead, drained, dried and stored in a plastic bag in the fridge.

Note that I use turkey or other animal fat as a final flavouring. This is a great technique to keep in mind when preparing a 'meat' side.

450g Brussels sprouts

kosher salt

2 tablespoons grapeseed or rapeseed oil

2 large shallots, finely sliced

60ml white wine

110g whole peeled chestnuts, cut into 0.5cm dice

1 tablespoon wholegrain mustard

2 tablespoons turkey, duck or chicken fat

Middle Eastern Courgette Cakes with Tahini Sauce

makes 25-30

Like most people, I love latkes, but the traditional kind is a carb-fest – and not exactly light. This delicious all-courgette version began when I was experimenting with Middle Eastern spices for Hannukah meal making. Tantalisingly flavoured, the cakes are accompanied by a garlicky tahini sauce that you could also use for lamb kebabs. The cakes are so good, I've been known to make a meal of them with just a salad and some simple grilled fish.

Geila's Tips

You can keep the cakes warm, if necessary, on the rack on which they drain (minus the kitchen paper, of course) in a preheated low oven.

The tahini sauce can be prepared ahead of time and refrigerated. Serve it chilled (as the recipe directs) or at room temperature.

900g courgettes, trimmed

kosher salt

3 small shallots, finely chopped

2 large garlic cloves, finely chopped

½ teaspoon ground cumin

2 tablespoons extra-virgin olive oil

½ teaspoon baking powder

65g plain flour, plus extra

1 medium egg

120ml rapeseed oil, for frying

Tahini Sauce

8 tablespoons tahini, well stirred

2 tablespoons orange juice or
1 tablespoon lemon juice

3 garlic cloves, finely chopped

1 teaspoon cumin

2 tablespoons chopped coriander
or flat-leaf parsley

½ teaspoon kosher salt

1. Place a colander in the sink. Using a food processor or hand grater, shred the courgettes and transfer to the colander (or grate directly into it). Sprinkle the courgettes generously with the salt. Allow them to exude liquid, about 20 minutes, then squeeze them with your hands or in a kitchen towel to remove as much remaining liquid as you can.

2. Transfer the courgettes to a large bowl and add the shallots, garlic and cumin. Taste and season with salt, if necessary. Mix well and stir in the olive oil, baking powder, flour and egg.

3. Flour your hands lightly and form the mixture into 24 balls about 5cm in diameter. Flatten the balls and place on a plate. (The courgettes can be made ahead and refrigerated for 2-3 hours.)

4. To make the tahini sauce, combine all the ingredients plus 60-80ml water in a medium bowl or hand blender beaker, and blend with a hand blender until the consistency reaches a thick cream. Alternatively, use an ordinary blender. If the mixture seems too thick, add more water by the tablespoon, blending after each addition. Adjust the seasoning and chill, if desired.

5. In a large frying pan, heat the rapeseed oil over a medium heat until a bit of the courgette mixture immediately sizzles when added. Add the courgette cakes and sauté until golden on the bottom, about 2 minutes. Turn, press to flatten and sauté about 1 minute more. Reduce the heat to medium-low and cook until the cakes are done through, 5-8 minutes, turning once. Meanwhile, place kitchen paper on a wire rack. When the cakes are done, transfer them to the rack and blot the tops with additional kitchen paper. Serve hot with the sauce on the side.

Savoury Flan Two Ways:
Velvet Parmesan
serves 8

I love the silky creaminess of a flan, so pleasing on the tongue. For years I experimented with savoury versions to be served as a side. This was my first success, a cheesy, custard-like dish that perfectly partners any grilled or poached fish, and it's very easy to make. You can also substitute this for the hollandaise in my Sole-Wrapped Asparagus with Hollandaise (page 77).

75–80g grated Parmesan
⅛ teaspoon cayenne
480ml dairy béchamel (page 196)
kosher salt and white pepper
2 medium eggs

1. Preheat the oven 170ºC/gas mark 3. Spray a 21.5 x 31.5cm baking dish with non-stick cooking spray, or grease it with butter.

2. Add the Parmesan and cayenne to the béchamel, and blend. Adjust the salt, if necessary, and season with pepper.

3. In a medium bowl, beat the eggs until well combined. Gradually add the béchamel mixture. Pour the mixture into the prepared baking dish, cover tightly with foil and transfer to a roasting pan. Add enough boiling water to the roasting pan to reach halfway up the sides of the baking dish. Transfer to the oven and bake until the flan is just set (the mixture will jiggle slightly when moved), 50–60 minutes. Check after 45 minutes.

4. Leave the flan to rest for 15 minutes, cut and serve.

Sweetcorn with Sage Flan
serves 8

Sweetcorn and I are like *this*. I'm always on the hunt for new ways to use it, and this flan is my latest discovery. Those who try this flan are often surprised that its creamy texture could be achieved without dairy ingredients, but that's indeed the case, thanks to the eggs and béchamel in it. This super-versatile dish can be served with just about any simply prepared meat or fish.

1. Preheat the oven to 180ºC/gas mark 4. Spray a 21.5 x 31.5cm baking dish with non-stick cooking spray.

2. In a medium frying pan, heat the oil over a medium-high heat. Add the onions and sauté, stirring, until lightly brown, about 6 minutes. Transfer the onions to a food processor, add the sweetcorn and sage leaves, and process until puréed. (Some chunks will remain.) Add the sugar, cayenne, salt and hazelnut oil, if using, and pulse to blend.

3. In a large bowl, combine the eggs and yolks, and beat. Add the béchamel to the sweetcorn mixture, blend thoroughly and adjust the seasoning, if necessary. Add the eggs, blend, and pour into the baking dish. Cover tightly with foil, and transfer to a roasting pan. Add enough boiling water to the roasting pan to reach halfway up the sides of the baking dish. Transfer to the oven and bake until a knife inserted in the flan comes out clean, about 60 minutes.

4. Leave the flan to rest for 15 minutes, cut and serve.

Convert it

To make this dairy, use dairy béchamel (page 196) instead of the pareve version, and butter instead of the grapeseed oil.

2 tablespoons grapeseed or rapeseed oil

1 medium onion, chopped

285g frozen sweetcorn, defrosted under hot tap water, drained

3 tablespoons chopped sage leaves, stems reserved

3 tablespoons sugar

¼ teaspoon cayenne

1 teaspoon kosher salt, plus more, if needed

1 tablespoon hazelnut oil (optional)

2 medium eggs plus 2 yolks

480ml pareve béchamel (page 196), warm

freshly ground black pepper, if needed

Parsnip Purée

serves 6

This couldn't-be-easier purée treats parsnips with the respect they deserve. Whenever I'm inclined to make mashed potatoes, I make this instead, and everyone is happy. More healthful than purées that contain butter or cream (or both), this is especially good with braised meats, whose rich sauces it soaks up enticingly.

Geila's Tip

Don't skip the parsnip-coring step; the fibrous vegetable interior prevents a creamy result.

900g parsnips

3 tablespoons extra-virgin olive oil

6 cloves roasted garlic

pinch nutmeg

1 teaspoon kosher salt

1. Peel, core and chop the parsnips into 1cm pieces. Transfer to a pan with enough cold water to cover them by 5cm, bring to the boil and cook until tender, 15-20 minutes.

2. Transfer the parsnips to a medium bowl and combine with the oil, garlic, nutmeg and salt. Purée with a hand blender or in a food processor. Adjust the seasoning, if necessary, and serve.

Glazed Shallots

serves 6–8

Traditionally, this dish of caramelised, sweet-and-tart roasted shallots took hours to make. But by glazing the shallots on the hob before roasting them, it's ready in minutes. Crispy on the outside, yielding on the inside, these go with just about any main dish. Use best-quality balsamic vinegar for this.

Geila's Tip

You can make these a day ahead. Roast the shallots for 10 minutes then cool and refrigerate them. Heat them directly from the fridge in a 200ºC/gas mark 6 oven for about 10 minutes.

3 tablespoons extra-virgin olive oil

2 tablespoons sugar

900g shallots

½ teaspoon kosher salt

3 tablespoons balsamic vinegar

2-3 tablespoons chopped parsley, for garnish

1. Preheat the oven to 190ºC/gas mark 5.

2. In a large ovenproof frying pan, combine the oil and sugar, and cook over a medium-high heat until the sugar melts, about 3 minutes. Add the shallots and toss to coat. Reduce the heat to medium and sauté the shallots, stirring occasionally, until golden, 5-7 minutes.

3. Sprinkle with the salt, add the vinegar and 240ml water, and deglaze the pan. Transfer the pan to the oven and roast the shallots until tender for 10-20 minutes, depending on size. Transfer to a serving dish, sprinkle with the parsley and serve.

Oven-Roasted New Potatoes

serves 8

Not every delicious dish needs to be complicated. This savoury side of crisp, garlicky potatoes almost makes itself. It's the perfect accompaniment to roast meats, chicken or fish – just about any main item. I like to season these with rosemary, but see other options in the ingredient listing.

1. Preheat the oven to 190ºC/gas mark 5. In a medium roasting pan, mix the potatoes and garlic. Add the salt, olive oil and rosemary, and toss.

2. Roast the potatoes until golden, about 45 minutes, stirring every 15–20 minutes to ensure even browning. Serve.

1.3kg unskinned new potatoes, preferably Anja potatoes

6 garlic cloves, flattened with the side of a knife

2 teaspoons sea salt

60ml extra-virgin olive oil

4 x 7.5cm fresh rosemary sprigs, 4 thyme sprigs, or 6g chopped flat-leaf parsley

chapter

Breakfast and Brunch

Breakfast and Brunch

Sometimes I think that brunch must be a Jewish invention. I mean, where would that happy occasion be without bagels, cream cheese and smoked salmon?

As beloved as that dish is, though, there's more to a.m. eating. Most breakfast and brunch dishes are dairy or sweet, categories I love recasting to make newly delicious fare.

My partiality is responsible for Crème Brûlée French Toast, a luscious cross of the perennial breakfast favourite and the rich dessert that's particularly appealing when sprinkled with fresh berries. It's also produced Matzo Brei with Caramelised Apples, a tantalising elevation of the customary favourite with the bonus of a pleasingly crunchy texture, and Nutella Banana Crêpes with Praline Crunch, a triple-whammy treat that gives the traditional filled-crêpe dish new life. My home-made schnecken are stellar breakfast eating and doable even for novice bakers. The inclusion of maple syrup in their filling sends those wonderful rolls heavenwards, though just their smell as they bake may be paradise enough.

I'm particularly pleased to present Sheila's Blintzes, the best version of the well-loved breakfast dish I've ever tried. I wouldn't dare mess with these, though I've included a technique for oven-finishing them that makes them easier to make for a crowd, and added a strawberry and blueberry filling variation that will delight your guests. The blintzes also offer cooks the opportunity to explore crêpe making, a skill that opens doors to many recipes, savoury as well as sweet.

What's new about Omelette Savoyard? Nothing. Stuffed with potatoes, onions and cheese, this frittata-like omelette, a peasant dish from the French Alps, is timeless for a reason. Guests devour it with relish, especially on cold winter mornings. If you haven't made it, you must. A classic you've never tried can be 'modern' too.

Nutella Banana Crêpes with Pralir

serves 6

This winning dish of Nutella-laced, banana-filled crêpes topped with v
began as a treat for my daughter. But when friends raved about it, I kne
particular will rejoice, as this really celebrates its chocolate-hazelnut s
whole presentation, make these without the praline or whipped crea

1. Spray a large sheet of baking paper with non-stick cooking spray.
Chill a medium bowl.

2. To make the praline, combine the sugar, corn syrup and 1 tablespoon
of water in a small saucepan, and heat over a medium-high, stirring.
When the sugar has dissolved, boil until the syrup is amber-coloured,
about 5 minutes. Remove from the heat, add the nuts, stir and pour the
mixture onto the baking paper. Using a spatula, spread the mixture into
a thin layer, and leave to cool completely, about 30 minutes. Break into
pieces, transfer to a food processor, and grind to make pea-sized chunks.

3. Next make the filling. In a large frying pan, combine the butter and
sugars, and cook over a medium-high heat until the sugars have melted
and the mixture is bubbling, 3-5 minutes. Whisk in the vanilla and rum
extract, if using, and cook for 2 more minutes. Remove from the heat,
and rapidly whisk in the cream. When the mixture begins to thicken,
add the bananas, return the pan to the hob and cook the bananas in
the caramel for 3 minutes. Using a sieve, drain the bananas, reserving
the caramel in a dish.

4. In the chilled bowl, whip the 225ml of cream until soft peaks form.
Add the 50g of sugar and continue to beat until stiff peaks form.
Refrigerate.

5. To assemble the crêpes, stir the Nutella and spread 1 tablespoon
from side to side on a crêpe. Top with 2 tablespoons of the banana,
and fold by lifting one side of the crêpe to cover the filling and folding
the opposite side over the first. Top with the whipped cream, sprinkle
with the praline and serve.

Pra.

100g suga.

1 teaspoon corn s,

50g chopped pecans

Filling

4 tablespoons unsalted butter

65g light brown soft sugar

65g sugar

1 teaspoon vanilla extract

1 teaspoon rum extract (optional)

55ml double cream

2 bananas, sliced into thirds,
cut into 1cm dice

225ml double cream

50g sugar

½ recipe crêpes (page 193)

8 tablespoons Nutella, at room
temperature

Brûlée French Toast

...e served French toast that had a surprising – and delightful – texture like bread pudding. Here's my ...French toast that owes its tender, irresistible bite and rich flavour to a third dish, crème brulée. All you ...soak the bread in a luscious 'brûlée' mixture and then double-cook it – on the hob for colour, then in the ...to develop texture. Sprinkled with whatever berries are in season, the result is welcomed equally by the ...oung and their elders.

Convert It

To make this pareve, substitute almond cashew cream (see page 17) for the double cream.

Geila's Tip

If you want to pull out all the stops – and then some – make this with Chocolate Challah (see page 191).

2 large eggs

115ml double cream

4 tablespoons maple syrup or 50g sugar

1 teaspoon vanilla extract

8 x 2cm-thick slices challah

icing sugar, for dusting

1. Preheat the oven to 90°C. Line a medium baking tray with foil and set aside.

2. In a large, low-sided bowl or large baking dish, combine the eggs, cream, sugar and vanilla, and whisk to blend. Add the challah and press down on it to soak up the liquid, turn, and repeat. The bread will be very soft.

3. Heat a medium griddle or medium frying pan over a medium heat. Spray the pan lightly with the cooking spray or grease with kitchen paper dipped in the oil. Drain half the challah by shaking it carefully over the bowl, place on the griddle without crowding, and sauté until lightly brown, turning once, about 6 minutes. Transfer the challah to the baking tray. Repeat with the remaining challah.

4. Bake until the custard has set (the challah will be firm when pressed), 20–30 minutes. Sprinkle with the icing sugar and serve.

Matzo Brei with Caramelised Apples

serves 4-6

Matzo brei is Jewish soul food. I'm reminded of that when friends invited for brunch invariably demand it. This recipe not only produces great matzo brei but also features an apple-maple accompaniment, based on the caramelised topping of Tarte Tatin, that makes this special. Diners also love the brei's non-traditional crunchy texture, achieved by pouring boiling water over the matzos to soften them, rather than giving them a soak.

1. In a large frying pan, melt the butter over a medium-high heat. Add the sugar, ½ teaspoon of cinnamon and the syrup, if using, and stir to blend. Add the apples and sauté, stirring frequently, until the apples have softened and the pan liquid is syrupy, 10–15 minutes. Set aside.

2. Boil a kettle of water. Place the matzos in a colander and pour the boiling water over them to soften them. Drain the matzos and press them against the colander to remove excess water.

3. In a large bowl, beat the eggs. Add the remaining ½ teaspoon of cinnamon, salt and the matzos, and stir to combine.

4. In a large frying pan, heat the oil over medium-high. Add the matzo mixture, flatten with a spatula to fill the pan evenly, and cook until the bottom has set, 4–5 minutes. Slip the matzo brei onto a plate and invert the plate over the pan. Cook until the eggs have set on the second side, about 3 minutes. Slide onto a serving dish, top with the apple mixture and serve.

Convert It

To make this pareve, substitute margarine for the butter.

Geila's Tip

To feed a crowd, double or triple the recipe. Spray a lasagne dish with non-stick cooking spray, spread the matzo mixture in it, and bake in a 180ºC/gas mark 4 oven for 20–25 minutes.

6 tablespoons unsalted butter

100g light brown soft sugar

1 teaspoon cinnamon

4 tablespoons pure maple syrup (optional)

5 Granny Smith apples, peeled, cored, sliced 0.5cm thick

4 matzos, broken into 5–7.5cm pieces

4 medium eggs

½ teaspoon kosher salt

1 tablespoon grapeseed or rapeseed oil

Schnecken
makes 12

Home-made schnecken – the name is German for snails, whose shell shape these sweet rolls imitate – excite everyone. As they bake, they fill the house with the scent of butter, cinnamon and caramelised sugar – and then comes that first-bite thrill. My version features maple syrup in the nut-strewn topping, which takes the rolls to a whole new level. Even novice bakers enjoy making these rolls, as no special skills are required.

Dough

7g active dried yeast

50g plus 1 tablespoon sugar

425–500g strong flour, as needed

½ teaspoon kosher salt

6 tablespoons unsalted butter, melted

8 tablespoons milk

115ml double cream

2 medium eggs

Topping

10 tablespoons unsalted butter, softened

50g light brown soft sugar

5 tablespoons pure maple syrup

130g chopped walnuts, pecans and/or skinned hazelnuts

Filling

300g light brown soft sugar

50g sugar

1 tablespoon cinnamon

Glaze

1 medium egg

2 tablespoons double cream

1. First make the dough. In a small bowl or measuring jug, combine the yeast and 1 tablespoon of sugar with 60ml of warm (40ºC) water. Stir and allow to rise until the mixture has doubled in size, 10–20 minutes.

2. In the bowl of a stand mixer fitted with the beater attachment, combine the flour, salt and remaining 50g of sugar. In a small bowl, combine the butter, milk, cream and eggs, and blend. Add the liquid mixture to the mixer bowl and mix at medium speed until well combined. Replace the beater with the dough hook and knead for 5 minutes, adding more flour if necessary to achieve a smooth, elastic dough. Transfer the dough to an oiled medium bowl, cover with cling film, and leave to rise until doubled in bulk, about 60 minutes.

3. Meanwhile, make the topping. Grease a 23 x 33cm baking dish. In a small bowl, combine the butter and light brown soft sugar. Beat in the syrup and nuts. Transfer to the baking dish and spread evenly.

4. Next, make the filling. In a small bowl, combine the sugars and the cinnamon, mix, and toss with the nuts. Set aside.

5. Preheat the oven to 180ºC/gas mark 4. Punch down the dough in the bowl and leave to rest for 10 minutes.

6. Turn the dough onto a work surface and roll into a 23 x 45cm rectangle. In a small bowl, combine the glaze ingredients, and brush over the dough. Sprinkle evenly with the filling. Starting with the long end nearest to you, roll up the dough like a Swiss roll. Slice the roll into 4cm pieces and arrange on top of the topping in the baking dish, spacing the pieces evenly and leaving sufficient room between them to allow them to rise. Set aside for 20 minutes.

7. Meanwhile, cover a large baking sheet with baking paper and set aside. Bake the schnecken until golden, 20–25 minutes, and invert onto the baking paper. Scrape out any topping that remains in the bowl and distribute evenly over the schnecken. Leave to cool before serving.

Omelette Savoyard

serves 4

This French classic – a frittata-like omelette filled with potatoes, onions and cheese that originated in the peasant kitchens of Savoy – may be the ultimate brunch dish. People love its hearty flavour – and it's easily made, as it's all done in a single pan. I like to serve the omelette moist, but you can cook it to the texture you prefer. Offer this with a mixed baby leaf salad and you'll be in business.

Geila's Tips

You can prepare the potatoes and onions in advance and refrigerate them. Before making the omelette, bring them to room temperature.

If you don't have a frying pan with an ovenproof handle, wrap your handle with foil before putting it in the oven.

225g Charlotte potatoes, unpeeled, cut into 0.5cm dice

2 teaspoons kosher salt, plus more

2 tablespoons grapeseed or rapeseed oil

1 tablespoon unsalted butter

1 onion, finely sliced

8 medium eggs

3 tablespoons double cream (optional)

80g grated hard cheese, such as Swiss or Gruyère

80g semi-soft cheese, such as raclette or havarti

2 tablespoons chopped parsley (optional)

1. In a 23cm frying pan with an ovenproof handle, combine the potatoes, 240ml of water and 1 teaspoon of salt. Bring to the boil over a medium-high heat and simmer until fork-tender, 8-10 minutes. Drain the potatoes and transfer to a plate.

2. In the same frying pan, heat 1 tablespoon of the oil and the butter. When the butter stops foaming, add the onion, sprinkle with a pinch of salt, and sauté until the onions are golden, 5-7 minutes. Return the potatoes to the pan to reheat, then transfer everything to a plate, and set aside.

3. In a medium bowl, beat the eggs with 1 teaspoon of salt until blended. Add the cream, if using.

4. Position an oven rack in the top third of the oven. Preheat the grill.

5. In the pan, heat the remaining oil over medium-high until hot but not smoking. Add half the egg mixture, swirl and cook the eggs until three-quarters done to your liking, about 3 minutes for still runny. Distribute the hard cheese over the eggs, leaving a 1cm border. Spread the potato mixture over, top with the soft cheese and pour the remaining egg mixture over. Place the pan under the grill and cook for 3 minutes, or 4-5 minutes if you like your eggs dry. Invert the omelette onto a serving dish, cover with foil and leave to rest for 5 minutes. Sprinkle with the parsley, if using, cut into wedges and serve.

Sheila's Blintzes
for 16 crêpes

Once a year my normally diet-conscious family gathers on Shavuot, the harvest festival that celebrates the giving of the Torah, for a calorie-defying blintz debauch. This version of those cheese-filled crêpes is from my mother's friend Sheila, whose blintzes are the world's best. My contributions are a technique for finishing the blintzes in the oven, which makes serving them for a gathering easy (see the Tip), and a filling variation featuring strawberries or blueberries. Passed around with a variety of accompaniments, these are heavenly.

1. Place a colander in a sink. Place the curd cheese in the colander and allow to drain for 15 minutes. Double a large sheet of kitchen paper, turn the cheese onto it, enclose it in the paper and press it to extract more liquid.

2. In a medium bowl, combine the curd cheese, cream cheese, sugar, egg, vanilla, zest and wheatgerm, if using. Beat until the mixture is fairly smooth.

3. Place a crêpe, darker side up, on a work surface. Place 2 tablespoons of the filling in the centre. To form the blintz, fold the nearest side over to cover the filling, fold the sides towards the centre, then fold again to 'close' the blintz. Transfer to a dish, seam side down. Repeat with the remaining crêpes and filling.

4. In a medium frying pan, heat the oil and butter over a medium heat until the butter stops foaming. Working in batches, and adding more oil and butter if needed, fry the blintzes seam side down until golden, about 3 minutes. Turn and repeat on the second side. Transfer the blintzes to kitchen paper as they're cooked. (You can keep them warm in the oven, if necessary.)

5. Transfer the blintzes to serving plates. Dust with icing sugar, if using, and serve with the accompaniment(s) of choice.

Variation:

For strawberry or blueberry blintzes, make the filling without the sugar. In a glass measuring jug, melt 145g of strawberry or blueberry jam in the microwave for 30 seconds. Alternatively, melt it in a small saucepan over a low heat. Allow the jam to cool before mixing into the filling. For a sweeter filling, add sugar by teaspoons to taste. Form the blintzes and proceed as above.

Geila's Tip

To make these for a crowd, line a baking sheet with baking paper and brush with 2 tablespoons of melted butter. Place the formed blintzes on it, seam side down, and brush the tops with 2 more tablespoons of melted butter. Bake in a preheated 180°C/gas mark 4 oven until golden, about 10 minutes.

450g unsalted curd cheese

115g cream cheese

50g sugar

1 medium egg

1 tablespoon vanilla extract

1 tablespoon grated lemon zest (optional)

100g wheatgerm (optional)

1 recipe crêpes (page 193)

1 tablespoon grapeseed or rapeseed oil, plus more, if needed

1 tablespoon unsalted butter, plus more, if needed

icing sugar, for dusting (optional)

sour cream, maple syrup and/or fresh fruit, such as berries or sliced peaches, for serving

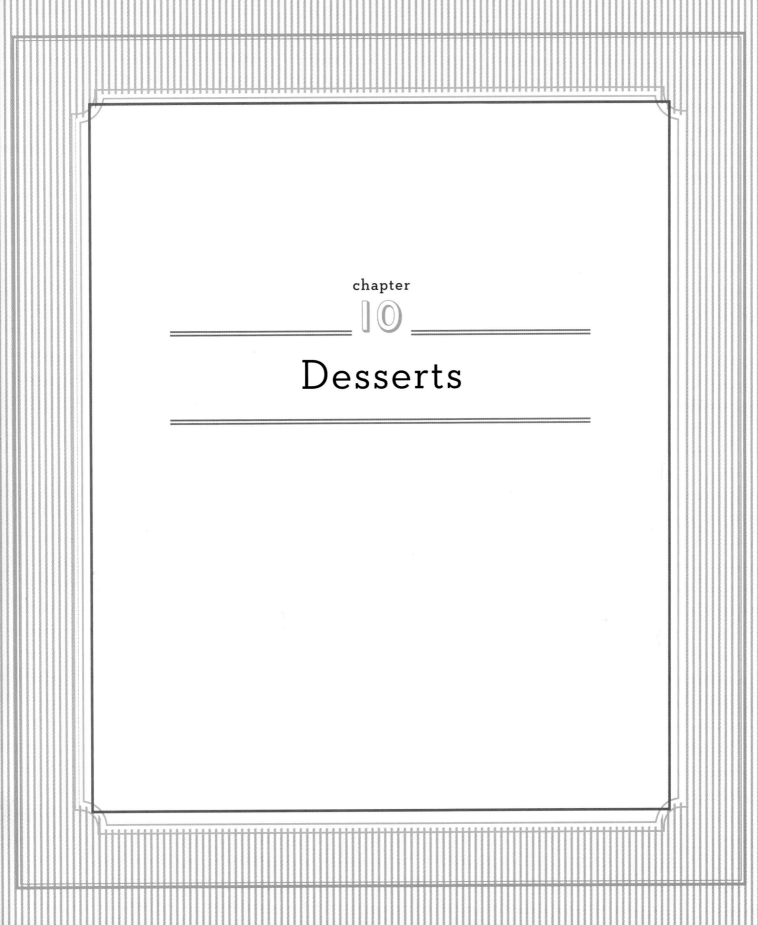

chapter

10

Desserts

Desserts

The kosher dessert repertoire is richly diverse. Even so, kosher dessert makers can feel their their options are limited. How to create great non-dairy sweets from recipes that depend on milk, butter or cream? How to make Passover desserts that deliver all the satisfaction of their everyday counterparts? 'Modern' thinking can help!

For converting dairy sweets to non-dairy ones, nut milks rule. Since their kosher certification, we no longer need rely on ersatz 'creams' to provide pareve creaminess. Similar in their fat and protein profiles to dairy milks, nut milks' natural sweetness also makes them ideal for dairy dessert recasting. For example, coconut milk helps to make a lusciously creamy pareve version of Crème Brûlée that's every bit as delicious as the dairy kind; it performs similarly to make the filling of Macadamia Raspberry Tart alluringly lush.

Margarine has had a loveless career, but works beautifully in the pareve version of Everyday Banana Cake, a household staple; in Maple Pecan Pie, a traditional favourite enhanced with maple syrup; and in Almond Crescents, terrific pareve bites that people can't get enough of.

Eggs are central to sweet making – they bind, moisten and act as a leavening, a talent Passover bakers put to good use. Eggs make Blueberry Lemon-Curd Sponge Cake light and are responsible for French Macarons, an elegant sandwich biscuit that can be tricky to make, but which I've demystified for home cooks. Egg-risen Chocolate Walnut Meringues take the usual Passover meringue biscuit to a much higher place, and can be fun to make with kids.

Speaking of chocolate, I couldn't write this chapter without including really serious chocolate desserts. Chocolate Soufflé Roll with Hazelnut Cream and Lava Cakes, with their molten chocolate centres, are guaranteed to make chocolate lovers very, very happy. The roll was created for Passover and should definitely settle the question of whether Passover desserts can be as tempting as the everyday kind. They can.

Lava Cakes

serves 6–8

Who doesn't love rich chocolate cake with a gooey chocolate centre? There's just enough flour in these aptly named ramekin-sized cakes to give them a bit of body, so you know you're eating cake, not mousse. Otherwise, they're molten lusciousness. Finish them with just a sprinkling of icing sugar, or serve them with whipped cream, ice cream or any complementary dessert sauce.

Convert It

To make these pareve, substitute margarine for the butter.

Geila's Tip

These can be assembled, frozen and baked later, directly from the freezer. Just add two minutes to the indicated baking time.

140g dark chocolate

10 tablespoons unsalted butter

3 medium eggs plus 3 yolks

100g icing sugar

45g plain flour

1. Preheat the oven to 230°C/gas mark 8. Spray eight 125ml or six 175ml ramekins with non-stick cooking spray. Set aside.

2. In a medium glass bowl, combine the chocolate and butter, and melt in the microwave, stirring every 30 seconds, for about 1½ minutes. Stir until smooth and set aside.

3. In the bowl of a stand mixer, or in a medium bowl, combine the eggs and yolks, and beat at medium speed, or by hand, until well combined, about 2 minutes if using a mixer. Add the sugar and beat until thick, about 3 minutes. Add the chocolate mixture, beat, add the flour, and beat until just combined. Spoon the mixture into the ramekins, place onto a baking sheet and bake until set but still soft in the middle, 8–10 minutes for 125ml ramekins, 10–12 minutes for 175ml ramekins. Cool for 1 minute, run a knife around the edges of the cakes, invert onto dessert plates and serve with an accompaniment, if using.

Everyday Banana Cake

serves 10–12

This banana cake is so popular in my house, I always have one in the freezer. Beautifully moist and with a pleasingly dense crumb, this walnut-studded version is the best I've tried. It's perfect for daily snacking or as a finish to a rich meal.

---

1. Cut a piece of baking paper to fit a 23cm cake tin and grease the paper. Set aside.

2. Sift the flour, baking powder, bicarbonate of soda and salt into a medium bowl. Set aside.

3. In the bowl of a stand mixer, combine the sugar and butter, and beat on medium speed until creamed, 2–3 minutes. Add the vanilla and blend. Add the eggs, reduce the speed to low, add the flour mixture gradually, and beat just until completely incorporated. Do not over-beat. Add the bananas and blend. Stir in the chopped walnuts, if using, and pour the batter into the cake tin. Arrange the walnut haves in a flower-petal pattern, 6 in the centre and 12 around the cake's edge.

4. Bake until a skewer inserted in the middle of the cake comes out clean, 45–60 minutes. If the top of the cake appears to be browning too quickly after 30 minutes, cover it loosely with foil. Run a knife around the cake's edge, invert onto a rack, then invert again onto a second rack so the top is face up. Cool before serving.

Convert It

To make this pareve, substitute margarine for the butter.

Geila's Tip

If you've got bananas on hand that are too ripe to eat, freeze them. When you've accumulated enough, defrost and drain them, then use them to make this cake.

260g flour

¾ teaspoon baking powder

1 teaspoon bicarbonate of soda

pinch salt

200g sugar

10 tablespoons unsweetened butter

1 tablespoon vanilla extract

2 medium eggs

4 large or 5 medium very ripe bananas, mashed

100g chopped walnuts or pecans, plus 18 haves (optional)

Blueberry Lemon-Curd Sponge Cake
serves about 12

Like many kosher cooks, I've made my share of sponge cakes, so-so, good and better. This one evolved from my wish to make an exceptional holiday version. My potchkying began with the addition of lemon zest. A year later I added a layer of rich and tangy lemon curd, followed, a year after that, by a blueberry garnish. I think you'll find the result of my tinkering as special as I do. This is the perfected Passover dessert that's also great for tea, a summer lunch or a picnic.

1. Preheat the oven to 180°C/gas mark 4. Grease a 25.5cm cake tin with a hole in the centre and with a removable base.

2. In a medium bowl, beat the egg whites until stiff but not dry. Set aside.

3. In the bowl of a stand mixer, combine the yolks and sugar, and beat on high speed until smooth and fluffy. Add the lemon juice and combine. Add the matzo meal, starch, salt and lemon zest and blend. Remove the bowl from the mixer and fold in the whites a third at a time. Pour the batter into the prepared cake tin and bake until a skewer inserted in the centre comes out clean, about 60 minutes. Cool for 10 minutes, run a knife around the cake and remove on the tin base. Finish cooling on the base.

4. Meanwhile, make the lemon curd. In a mini food processor, combine the sugar and lemon-zest, and pulse until combined. Fill a small saucepan two-thirds full with water and bring to a simmer over a medium heat. In a non-porous bowl, combine the yolks, sugar and zest mixture, lemon juice and starch, place over but not touching the water, and whisk until it thickens to the consistency of a light mixture, about 4 minutes. Remove the mixture from the heat and add the margarine, stirring to blend. Sieve the mixture into a small bowl, cover with cling film so it touches the top of the curd, and refrigerate for at least 2 hours or overnight.

5. Make a simple syrup. In a small saucepan, combine 150g sugar and 180ml water and bring to the boil over a medium heat, stirring until the sugar dissolves completely, about 3 minutes. Alternatively, combine the sugar and water in a 500ml measuring jug, and microwave until the syrup forms, stirring the mixture every 30 seconds, about 3 minutes. Chill.

6. Remove the cake from the tin base and halve horizontally. With a pastry brush, brush away any crumbs. Brush the cut side of the bottom layer and the top of the upper layer with the syrup, and set aside for 20 minutes (to allow the syrup to seal the cake).

7. Place the bottom layer on a cake plate and spread with the curd evenly, about 0.5cm thick. Top with the upper layer, and ice the top of the cake with the remaining curd. Fill the centre of the cake with some of the blueberries and arrange the remaining ones around the base of the cake on the platter. Dust with icing sugar and serve.

Convert It

To make this dairy, substitute butter for the margarine in the lemon curd.

9 medium eggs, separated
300g sugar
60ml lemon juice
130g fine matzo meal
25g potato starch
pinch of kosher salt
grated zest of 1 lemon

Lemon Curd
100g sugar
grated zest of 3 lemons
6 medium egg yolks
120ml lemon juice
2 teaspoons potato starch
8 tablespoons margarine, cut into 1cm dice

To Decorate
150g sugar
125g blueberries
icing sugar, for dusting

Chocolate Soufflé Roll with Hazelnut Filling

for one 40.5cm roll

I created this marvellous roll for Passover. After its appearance elicited many oohs and aahs, followed by a blissed-out silence once diners had dug in, I decided this dessert was too good for holidays only. The combination of chocolate and hazelnuts is one of those things made in heaven.

Convert It

To make this a dairy dish, use butter in place of the margarine.

Geila's Tip

You can make the filling in advance, refrigerate it, then bring it to room temperature for the right spreading consistency.

225g dark chocolate (check the label to ensure it's pareve)

80ml hazelnut liqueur, port or water

3 tablespoons unsalted butter or margarine

8 medium eggs, separated

pinch kosher salt

100g sugar

Filling

4 medium egg whites

200g sugar

225g margarine, softened

115g praline paste

1 teaspoon hazelnut extract

icing sugar, for dusting or 50g each of dark and white chocolate chips, melted, for drizzling

1. Preheat the oven to 180°C/gas mark 4. Place an oven rack at the middle level. Grease a baking sheet, line with baking paper, then grease the paper.

2. Finely chop the chocolate. In a small heatproof bowl, combine the chocolate with the liqueur and butter. Place the bowl over a saucepan of hot water, without the bowl touching the water, and stir occasionally until the chocolate is melted and the mixture is smooth. One at a time, beat in the yolks.

3. Combine the salt and the egg whites and beat until they're just beginning to hold a very soft peak. Add the sugar in a slow stream, beating faster. Stir a quarter of the egg whites into the chocolate mixture, then fold the chocolate mixture into the whites.

4. Pour the batter onto the baking sheet and smooth the top with a spatula. Bake until firm to the touch, about 15 minutes. Remove from the oven and loosen the cake by working a small knife along its sides. Pulling on the paper, slide the cake onto a work surface to cool, about 20 minutes.

5. Meanwhile, make the filling. Fill a saucepan with water and bring to a simmer over a medium heat. Place a metal bowl from a stand mixer (or use a metal bowl with a hand mixer) over the saucepan, add the egg whites and sugar, and whisk gently until the mixture has reached a temperature of 76°C, 6-8 minutes. Place the bowl on the mixer (or off the heat if using a hand mixer) and beat on high speed until a stiff, glossy meringue forms and the mixture has cooled somewhat. Fold in the butter by hand until completely incorporated. Fold in the praline paste and hazelnut extract. Chill the filling until it has stiffened slightly.

6. To finish the roll, slide a rimless baking sheet under the layer. Cover the layer with a clean sheet of baking or greaseproof paper and another sheet the same size as the first. Invert the sheets, remove the top (formerly the bottom) sheet and peel off the paper. Invert again and remove the top sheet and remaining paper.

7. With a metal spatula, spread the filling onto the layer. Roll the layer by picking up one long edge of the paper and easing the layer into a curve. Continue lifting the paper while rolling the cake. Roll the cake onto a platter, seam side down. Sprinkle with icing sugar and serve.

Maple Pecan Pie
serves 8

Every so often I get a pecan pie urge, which, for me, means I need to make one. On one such occasion I discovered I didn't have corn syrup, the pie's traditional sweetener. The serendipitous replacement was maple syrup, which adds it own great flavour as well as sweetness. I also used a shop-bought frozen pastry case – my standard back-up when making this, especially when it's part of a big-deal holiday menu. Feel free, of course, to make your own case, but a bought one works beautifully here and saves tons of time. Using chopped and whole pecans adds textural interest.

Convert It

To make this dairy, use unsalted butter in place of the margarine.

---

1 x 23cm frozen pastry case

300g pecans, 200g coarsely chopped, the remainder whole

1 tablespoon plain flour

250ml pure maple syrup

150g packed light brown soft sugar

50g sugar

3 medium eggs

3 tablespoons margarine, melted

1 teaspoon vanilla extract

1. Preheat the oven to 180ºC/gas mark 4.

2. Cover a baking sheet with foil and place the pastry case onto it. Spread the chopped nuts over the case and arrange the whole nuts on top. Set aside.

3. In a medium bowl, combine the flour, syrup, sugars, eggs, margarine and vanilla. Stir to blend and pour over the nuts. Bake until the filling is set and slightly puffed, about 60 minutes. Transfer to a rack to cool before serving.

Allie's Apple Cake

serves 12–16

Allie is my mum. When I started to take cooking seriously, my mum – a great cook – passed the cooking baton on to me, which made me proud. But some dishes are still hers, like this rustic, dense-but-moist, apple-rich cake. No matter how many desserts I turn out for a holiday dinner, arriving guests invariably ask, 'Did Allie make her cake?' When she has and I tell them so, they immediately say, 'Can I take some home?' Need I say more?

1. Preheat the oven to 190ºC/gas mark 5. Oil a 25.5cm cake tin with a hole in the centre.

2. In a medium bowl, combine the apples, cinnamon, raisins and 50g of sugar. Stir and set aside.

3. In a second medium bowl, combine the flour, baking powder, remaining 400g of sugar, vanilla, eggs, oil and orange juice, and stir to blend thoroughly. Pour a quarter of this batter into the prepared cake tin and layer with a third of the apple mixture. Continue to layer the batter and apples, ending with batter. Bake until a skewer inserted into the cake comes out clean, about 80 minutes. Check every 30 minutes to ensure the cake isn't browning too quickly. If it is, cover loosely with foil.

4. Unmould onto a rack, invert so the cake top is face up, and cool. Cut and serve.

170–225g Granny Smith apples, peeled, cored and cut into 0.5cm slices

2 teaspoons cinnamon

70g raisins

450g sugar

400g plain flour

3 teaspoons baking powder

2 tablespoons vanilla extract

4 medium eggs

240ml rapeseed oil

120ml orange juice

Macadamia Raspberry Tart

serves 10-12

Nothing is more delicious – or beautiful – than a raspberry tart. My pareve version tastes every bit as good as one made with milk or cream, thanks to nut milk. The tart also works very well for Passover, as the pastry is made from crunchy, flavourful macadamias. If you want to gild the lily, you can brush the inside of the pastry case with melted chocolate before adding the pastry cream layer, but the tart is wonderful as is.

Convert It

To make this a dairy dish, use milk in place of the coconut milk in the filling.

Geila's Tip

You can make the pastry cream in advance and store it in the fridge. If you do, be sure to use coconut milk, which helps to ensure that proper consistency is maintained. If the filling does break, make a paste from 1 tablespoon of cornflour mixed with 2 tablespoons of water. Heat the cream, stirring constantly, over a medium-low heat. Stir in the paste and keep stirring until the filling is smooth again.

Pastry

200g macadamia nut flour or other nut flour

1 egg yolk

2 tablespoons sugar

6 tablespoons margarine, softened

Filling

3 medium egg yolks

300ml coconut, almond or hazelnut milk

3 tablespoons potato starch or cornflour

70g sugar

1 teaspoon vanilla extract

70g raspberry jam

480g raspberries

icing sugar, for dusting

1. Spray a 23cm tart tin, preferably with a removable bottom, with non-stick cooking spray. Cut a 23cm circle from baking paper and line the bottom of the tin with it. Spray the paper and tin sides.

2. In a food processor, combine the nut flour, yolk, sugar and margarine, and process until a dough-like mixture forms. Transfer the mixture to the tin and, using a spatula or your fingers, spread evenly to cover the bottom and sides. Freeze for 1 hour.

3. Preheat the oven to 160ºC. Bake the pastry until it turns a very light brown, about 20 minutes, transfer to a rack and cool.

4. Meanwhile, make the filling. In a small saucepan, combine the egg yolks, 240ml of the nut milk, the starch, and half of the sugar. Set aside. In a small glass bowl, combine the remaining 60ml nut milk, the vanilla, and the remaining half of the sugar. Heat in the microwave until hot, about 1 minute. Alternatively, heat in a small saucepan over a medium heat.

5. Drop by drop, and stirring rapidly, add the hot liquid to the starch mixture. As the mixture becomes tempered, add the hot liquid more rapidly. Transfer to the hob and heat over a medium heat, stirring constantly. When the mixture begins to boil, after about 2 minutes, remove from the heat and stir until smooth. The mixture should have the consistency of a light custard. Immediately transfer it to a medium glass bowl and cover with cling film, allowing it to touch the top of the mixture. Refrigerate.

6. In a glass dish, heat the jam in the microwave to melt it, about 30 seconds. Alternatively, melt it in a small saucepan over a low heat, stirring. Brush the jam over the pastry and allow to cool to seal it. Spread the cream evenly on top. Arrange the berries in concentric circles on top, sprinkle with icing sugar and serve.

Apricot Strudel

makes about 60 pieces

These apricot-, nut- and raisin-filled bites have always been called strudel in my family, but they're actually a cross between that flaky treat and rugelach, the traditional Jewish rolled biscuits, which literally means 'little twists' in Yiddish. Equally perfect for dessert and nibbling, these treats disappear fast. You can vary the filling as you like, but if you do, be sure to keep the same ingredient ratio.

225g unsalted butter, softened

220g cream cheese

300g sifted flour

300g dried apricots

130g chopped walnuts

425g sultanas, or dried cranberries

1. In a medium bowl, combine the butter and cream cheese, and blend thoroughly. Add the flour and stir until the mixture forms a ball. Wrap in cling film and chill in the fridge for 3-4 hours or overnight.

2. Divide the pastry into 4 parts. Flour a work surface and roll 1 part into a 35 x 40cm rectangle. Spread with 75g of the dried apricots, and sprinkle with 30g of the nuts and 100g of the raisins. Roll the pastry like a Swiss roll, and gently flatten to create an oval shape. Repeat with the remaining three pieces of pastry and the rest of the ingredients. Transfer to an ungreased baking sheet and freeze until solid, about 2 hours.

3. Preheat the oven to 175ºC. Thaw the rolls for 15 minutes and, using a serrated knife, cut them into 1cm slices. Transfer the slices to 2 baking sheets and bake until golden brown, about 45 minutes.

Almond Crescents

makes about 40

One day my pal Deborah presented me with these biscuits to taste. Having tried many an almond crescent in my time, I put on my polite face and took a bite. But no pretence was needed – Deborah's crescents have all the rich flavour of a butter biscuit and a superior crumb. In short, they're the best pareve nibble ever. This recipe is easy and works every time. I keep the dough in the freezer at all times so I can turn out a batch in minutes.

Convert It

To makes these dairy, substitute butter for the margarine.

Geila's Tip

You can make these in a standard biscuit shape. Just roll the dough into balls about 2.5cm in diameter, flatten them and bake.

1. Position an oven rack in the upper third of the oven. Preheat the oven to 180ºC/gas mark 4. Line a baking sheet with baking paper.

2. In a food processor, chop the nuts until finely ground. Do not over-process - they should remain powdery.

3. In the bowl of a stand mixer, combine the margarine, sugar and almond extract, and beat on high speed until creamed, 2-3 minutes. Add the ground almonds, reduce the speed to low, and gradually add the flour, mixing until a ball is formed. Transfer the mixture to a work surface and knead lightly until the dough coheres.

4. Pinch off 1-tablespoon pieces of the dough and roll into 5cm cigar shapes. Bend each into a crescent and transfer to the prepared baking sheet. Bake until just beginning to colour, about 15 minutes. Transfer to a rack, cool, and dust with icing sugar before serving.

65g blanched almonds

10 tablespoons margarine

70g sugar

½ teaspoon almond extract

270g flour, sifted

icing sugar, for dusting

Chocolate Walnut Meringues
makes 16

These classic biscuits are often the first baking test for many savoury cooks, as they're easy to do as well as delicious. For exactly those reasons, I make them often. This version is beautifully crispy, thanks to the use of caster sugar. For convenience, you can dry the baked meringues in the turned-off oven overnight. Just don't turn on the oven the next morning, as I've done, without removing them first!

1. Preheat the oven to 110ºC/gas mark ¼. Line two baking sheets with baking paper or aluminium foil, shiny side up.

2. In the bowl of a stand mixer fitted with the whisk attachment, combine the egg whites and salt, and beat on medium speed until soft peaks are formed, 2-3 minutes. Add the vanilla and, when incorporated, add the sugar in eight additions, beating for 1 minute between additions. When all the sugar is added, increase the speed to high and beat until the meringue is without any sugar feel when rubbed between your fingers, 3-5 minutes.

3. Remove the bowl from the mixer and fold in the chocolate and walnuts. Spoon 8-10cm mounds of the meringue onto the prepared baking sheets and bake until dry, reversing the sheets halfway through, front to back, and also exchanging one for the other, about 2 hours.

4. Turn off the oven, but leave the meringues in to dry out completely, at least 90 minutes or overnight. Remove the meringues from the sheets and serve, or store in an airtight container for up to two weeks.

Geila's Tips

These are great beginner biscuits to make with kids as they are fairly simple to create.

You could also substitute the walnuts with other types of nuts. Hazelnuts and pistachios both work extremely well.

120ml egg whites (from about 4 medium eggs), at room temperature

pinch kosher salt

1½ teaspoons vanilla extract

200g caster sugar

100g dark chocolate, chopped into 0.5cm dice

65g chopped walnuts (optional)

Crème Brûlée

serves 4

The availability of nut milks with kosher certification has meant that crème brulée, the ultimate dairy dessert, can now be made pareve. The lush texture of this recasting suggests the inclusion of double cream, but coconut milk is used instead. I love the subtle coconut flavour of this version, not to mention its crackly burnt-sugar topping, and I think you will too.

1. Transfer the coconut milk to a 500ml measuring jug and stir well to mix the liquid and fat. Add the vanilla bean halves, or vanilla extract, and microwave until almost boiling, 1–2 minutes, stirring after 1 minute and every 30 seconds thereafter. Alternatively, heat in a small saucepan over a medium-low heat until almost boiling. Set aside.

2. Place four ramekins in a small baking dish. Preheat the oven to 180ºC/ gas mark 4.

3. Fill a medium saucepan, or double boiler bottom, two-thirds full with water and bring to a simmer over a medium heat. Place the sugar and eggs in a bowl or double boiler top, and whisk over – but not touching – the simmering water until the yolks begin to lighten and the mixture is no longer gritty. Remove the pods, if using, from the milk and start adding it drop by drop to the yolk mixture, stirring constantly until heated, about 2 minutes. Pour the mixture into the ramekins, transfer to the oven, and pour enough hot water into the baking dish to reach halfway up the sides of the ramekins. Bake until set but still slightly wobbly, 40–50 minutes. Remove the ramekins from the baking dish, allow to cool on the work surface for 1 hour, then chill for at least 3 hours.

4. Sprinkle the surface of the custards with sugar and use a kitchen blowtorch to caramelise the sugar by moving the flame evenly over the surfaces. Alternatively, preheat the grill, transfer the sugar-topped custards to a baking sheet and grill 2.5cm from the heat source until caramelised. Watch carefully to ensure that the sugar doesn't burn. Allow the custards to cool, then chill in the fridge for at least 15 minutes before serving.

Convert It

For the traditional dairy brulée, substitute double cream for the coconut milk and bake for 10 minutes less than indicated.

1 x 400ml tin full-fat coconut milk (not light)

1 vanilla pod, split and scraped, or 1 tablespoon vanilla extract

65g sugar plus more, for the glaze

5 medium egg yolks

Cranberry-Almond Biscotti

makes about 30

For a long time I faithfully baked mandelbrot, the traditional almond bread that's served like a biscuit. Then I was given a flavourful biscotti recipe from my friend Ron, and haven't looked back. This delicious version balances the biscuit's usual sweetness with tart dried cranberries. A touch of cream sherry adds its own flavour.

Geila's Tip

You can substitute sweet white wine for the sherry.

130g almonds

50g potato starch

100g fine matzo meal, plus extra for dusting

1 teaspoon baking powder

3 medium eggs

150g sugar

3 teaspoons cream sherry

90g dried cranberries

80g roughly chopped shelled unsalted pistachios or flaked almonds

1. Preheat the oven to 150ºC/gas mark 2. Line two baking sheets with baking paper.

2. In a mini food processor, grind the whole almonds as finely as possible. Transfer to a large bowl and add the starch, matzo meal and baking powder. Stir to combine well and set aside.

3. In the bowl of a stand mixer fitted with the whisk attachment, combine 2 eggs and the yolk from the third (reserve the extra white). Whisk on medium speed until you reach a light lemony colour. Gradually whisk in the sugar until fully incorporated, then whisk in the sherry, cranberries and flaked almonds. Reduce the speed to low, add the dry ingredients and stir until the mixture forms a firm but sticky dough.

4. Wet your hands, divide the dough into four portions and, working on the baking sheets, form each into an oblong roll about 35 x 5cm, making sure the ends are equal in thickness to the rest of the roll. Beat the reserved egg white and brush on the top and sides of each roll. Bake until the dough is firm, about 50 minutes. Transfer to a rack and cool, 10-15 minutes.

5. Place the rolls on a chopping board and, with a serrated knife, slice the rolls diagonally into 1cm pieces. Line the baking sheets with fresh baking paper and transfer the pieces on their sides to both sheets. Bake until dry, turning the biscotti once, about 40 minutes.

6. Transfer the biscotti to racks to cool. Serve, or store in airtight tins or in resealable plastic bags in the freezer for up to two months.

Pignoli Biscuits

makes 30

Years ago I had a date with a boy who brought me a box of pignoli biscuits from Little Italy in lower Manhattan. The biscuits were an instant hit (alas, he wasn't) and became a great favourite of mine. They're simple to make, pareve, and perfect for Passover. The nuts give the biscuits a buttery texture, so they seem rich, even though they're not, which is just what you want from a biscuit as addictive as these.

1. Preheat the oven to 170ºC/gas mark 3. Line two baking sheets with baking paper and set aside.

2. In a food processor, combine the almond paste and sugars, and process until the mixture reaches the consistency of sand. Transfer to the bowl of a stand mixer fitted with the flat beater attachment, or a medium bowl, and add the egg white, vanilla and almond extracts. Beat on medium speed or by hand for 4 minutes.

3. Place the pine nuts in a small bowl. Next to it place a small bowl of water for wetting your hands. Wet your hands and form 4-5cm balls with the paste mixture, making five at a time. Drop them into the bowl of nuts and press down gently so the nuts adhere to the bottom of the balls. Transfer to a baking sheet, nut side up. Repeat, filling each prepared baking sheet with about 15 balls. Bake until puffed and beginning to colour, 15-18 minutes. Remove from the oven, and cool on the baking paper on a work surface. When completely cool, peel the biscuits off the paper and serve.

225g almond paste

35g icing sugar

100g sugar

1 large egg white

1 teaspoon almond extract

1 teaspoon vanilla extract

130g pine nuts

Hamentashen with Four Fillings

makes 36

These triangular Purim treats are traditionally made with a poppy seed or prune filling, but nowadays they're available with other fillings, like apricot and raspberry. My own 'hamentashing' has resulted in the new and delicious fillings included here, such as dried cranberries with apricot and Nutella with coconut. Adding breadcrumbs to the fillings ensures that they stay put. These are easily made and are welcome all year round.

Geila's Tips

It's much easier to work with the dough and fillings when they're cold. I like to prepare everything the night before and form and bake the hamentashen the next day. (It's necessary to make and freeze the chocolate filling in advance.)

Pastry

340g flour, plus a little extra

1½ teaspoons baking powder

120ml rapeseed oil

150g sugar

1 tablespoon vanilla extract

2 medium eggs

1 tablespoon orange juice (optional)

Poppy Filling

55g poppy seeds

340g blackcurrant jam

70g raisins, soaked in boiling water until soft, drained

20g breadcrumbs

Raspberry Filling

340g raspberry jam

65g chopped walnuts

20g breadcrumbs

Apricot Filling

340g apricot jam

70g dried cranberries, soaked in boiling water until soft, drained

20g breadcrumbs

Coconut-Chocolate-Hazelnut Filling

1 x 370g jar Nutella, or other chocolate-hazelnut spread

70g flaked coconut

1. First make the pastry. Sift the flour and baking powder onto baking paper. In a bowl of a stand mixer fitted with the flat beater attachment, combine the oil, sugar and vanilla, and blend on medium speed. One at a time, add the eggs, incorporating the first before adding the second, and blend. Add the orange juice, if using, and blend. Reduce the speed and add the flour mixture gradually to make a pastry.

2. Divide the dough into two parts and flatten each to make a disc. Wrap each disc in cling film, stack the discs on a plate, and refrigerate until stiff enough to work easily, at least 2 hours.

3. Meanwhile, make the filling(s). For the poppy, raspberry and/or apricot fillings, combine the ingredients in small bowls, stir to blend, and refrigerate for 1 hour. For the chocolate filling, combine the ingredients in a small bowl. Transfer half the filling to the centre of a 45cm piece of cling film, fold the cling film over the filling to enclose it, and squeeze the mixture to create a roll 2.5cm in diameter. Repeat with the remaining filling and freeze the rolls.

4. Preheat the oven to 180ºC/gas mark 4. Flour a work surface well and roll one of the discs out on it. Using a 7.5cm glass or biscuit cutter, cut out rounds. Pipe about 1 tablespoon of the poppy, raspberry, and/or apricot filling(s) in the centre of each round, wet the edges with water and bring up the sides of the rounds to make a three-sided triangular shape. Pinch the dough together to seal. Alternatively, drop the filling onto the dough by heaping tablespoons. For the chocolate filling, cut the frozen rolls into 1cm discs. Fill the rounds by placing a disc in the centre of each, form and seal.

5. Transfer the hamentashen to one or more baking sheets and bake, in batches if necessary, until pale gold, 12-14 minutes. Transfer to a rack and cool.

French Macarons

makes 24-30

Don't confuse these glorious, slightly chewy mouthfuls, made from a few simple ingredients, with the more common coconut macaroons most of us know. Variously flavoured, and composed of two meringue biscuits sandwiched around a filling like chocolate ganache or lemon curd, they're rich yet delicate – a major treat. For years I struggled with the recipe, which can be tricky, until I finally devised this foolproof method. The secret is the use of ground almonds and proper mixture consistency. Just follow my instructions for sure success.

If not coloured by their flavouring, the meringues are usually tinted – red for a raspberry filling, for example. Directions for doing so are given, but feel free to leave the biscuits au naturel.

Geila's Tip

To make a disposable piping bag for piping all but the chocolate filling, use a resealable plastic bag from which you've cut out one bottom corner.

100g ground almonds

180g icing sugar

3 egg whites from medium eggs, at room temperature (ideally, kept out overnight)

50g sugar

few drops red or other food colouring, if desired

Flavouring Variations

50g cocoa powder OR

2 teaspoons vanilla extract, or the seeds from 1 vanilla pod OR

2 teaspoons coffee extract or raspberry extract

Filling Variations

chocolate ganache (recipe opposite)

lemon curd (page 167)

lime curd (page 167; substitute fresh lime juice for the lemon juice and add a few drops of green food colouring)

jam, such as raspberry, strawberry or blackcurrant

1. First make the macarons. In a food processor, combine the ground almonds and icing sugar, and process until well combined, 90 seconds. For the flavouring, if making chocolate macarons, add the cocoa powder to the blended mixture and stir. If making vanilla macarons with the vanilla pod, add the seeds. Pass the mixture through a fine sieve and set aside.

2. In the bowl of a stand mixer fitted with a whisk attachment, whisk the egg whites on high speed until they form soft peaks. Reduce the speed to low and slowly add the granulated sugar. Increase the speed to high and whisk until stiff, glossy peaks are formed, 90 seconds–2½ minutes. If using coffee or raspberry extract, and/or food colouring, add now. Add the ground almonds mixture all at once and whisk until the mixture is just well combined, about 10 seconds. Do not allow the mixture to get soupy. Check by dropping one teaspoon on a flat surface. The mixture should spread slightly, not thin out. Surface marks should dissolve into the mixture. If the mixture doesn't spread at all, give it a few more stirs, and test again.

3. Transfer the mixture to a pastry bag fitted with a 0.5cm tip. Line a baking sheet with baking paper. Anchor it at the corners with drops of the mixture. Pipe 4-5cm circles onto the paper. To do this easily, hold the bag at a 90-degree angle and squeeze it while keeping the tip stationary as the mixture spreads into a circle. Quickly lift the tip and form the next macaron. Let the macarons rest until their surfaces become dull and a crust forms, about 60 minutes.

4. Meanwhile, preheat the oven to 170ºC/gas mark 3. Bake the macarons until the tops are completely dry and the macarons come off the paper easily without leaving any residue, 15-20 minutes. Transfer the macarons while still on the paper to a work surface. Cool and remove from the paper.

To fill the macarons, turn them flat side down and pair them by matching size. Place 1-1½ teaspoons of filling on the bottom half of each pair, cover with the top half, and press to form a sandwich. The filling should be visible. Repeat with the remaining macaron pairs. Refrigerate for 60 minutes to set the filling. Bring to room temperature before serving.

Chocolate Ganache
makes 240ml

Convert It

To make this a pareve dish, substitute non-dairy cream for the double cream.

115g dark chocolate
115ml double cream

1. Grind the chocolate in a food processor. Place the cream in a small glass bowl and heat in the microwave for 30 seconds on high. Stir and heat for 30 seconds more. The cream should be very hot. Alternatively, heat the cream in a small saucepan over a medium heat until hot, about 3 minutes. Add the chocolate and stir until well blended. Refrigerate, stirring every 15 minutes, until cool and the consistency of frosting is reached, about 60 minutes. If the ganache becomes too solid to spread, microwave it for 5 seconds and stir, or heat it in a bowl over hot water for about 30 seconds.

chapter

II

Basics

Basics

This chapter helps you to create your own great recipes. It also introduces you to bread making, a skill that provides deep satisfaction to both the baker and those who enjoy wonderful bread.

Foundation recipes are called that for a reason. Crêpes, for example, help make possible a wide range of sweet and savoury dishes. They're easy to do and, once mastered, make it a cinch for you to produce such treats as Sheila's Blintzes (page 159), Nutella Banana Crêpes with Praline Crunch (page 151) or your own manicotti, which you can stuff with the filling used for Aubergine Rollatini (page 123).

No kosher store cupboard is complete without stocks. I'm pleased to offer an exceptional recipe for vegetable stock – it's deeply flavourful and clean tasting – and one for veal or beef stock, culinary money in the bank. The effort involved in producing it is repaid a zillion-fold when you need to add deep flavour to savoury dishes that would otherwise languish when made with commercial bouillons.

I'm particularly happy to present a recipe for paneer, the fresh, ricotta-like Indian cheese that I serve with cauliflower masala (page 120) and that also makes a great accompaniment to curried peas.

My own non-dairy version of béchamel is as creamy and rich as the traditional kind (a recipe for which I also supply), and makes possible a wide range of creamy pareve dishes, like Broccoli Soufflé (page 134) and Sweetcorn with Sage Flan (page 143). Sun-dried Tomato and Herb Dressing, a flavour-packed seasoning for cooked meats, is also great as a bread dip.

I came to bread making late, but once I did, I was hooked. As good as it is in itself, Classic Challah, for which I offer a superior recipe, was a point of departure, yielding tempting variations. Peshwari Challah, which is based on the Indian flatbread called peshwari naan, is filled with pistachios, raisins, coconut and sweet spices. It's easily done and makes a terrific accompaniment to soups and other savoury dishes. Chocolate Challah began as a treat for my daughter but has become an adult favourite too. It's a wonderful snack, but also makes a mean French toast, see Crème Brûlée French Toast (page 152). You'll consider it, and the other recipes in this chapter, basic to a well-stocked cooking life.

Classic Challah

makes 2 x 450g loaves

Bread making has always given me pleasure. It's odd, then, that it took me a while to make my own challah - which I did only after realising that I'd made all the dishes for a Rosh Hashanah dinner *except* the bread. This recipe, and the peshwari and chocolate variations that follow it, are the results of my wish to change that. If you're new to bread baking, or even an old hand at it, I urge you to try this recipe. It produces a golden, moist loaf with a beautifully layered crumb. The dough braiding comes naturally once you've done it, but if you'd prefer not to tackle it, go directly to the variations whose loaves are easier to form. Actually, you shouldn't miss the variations, which take challah in wonderful new directions.

2¼ teaspoons active dried yeast

480g-565g strong flour, as needed

1 tablespoon plus 70g sugar

1½ teaspoons kosher salt

3 medium eggs

120ml rapeseed oil

1. In a 250ml measuring jug, combine the yeast with 180ml of warm (about 40°C) water and the 1 tablespoon of sugar. Stir and leave to sit until about 2-3cm of foam has formed, about 10 minutes.

2. Meanwhile, in the bowl of a stand mixer fitted with the flat beater attachment, combine the 480g of flour, sugar and salt, and stir on low speed. Make a well in the centre of the mixture.

3. In a small bowl, combine 2 of the eggs and the oil, mix, and pour into the well. Expand the well, then pour in the yeast mixture. Mix briefly on low speed to combine. Remove the flat beater, insert the dough hook, sprinkle the mixture with 35g of flour, and knead on low speed for 1 minute. If the dough is still sticky, add more flour by 35g measures to achieve a soft, unsticky dough. Continue to knead for a total of 5 minutes. Alternatively, to form the dough by hand, put the dry ingredients in a large bowl, make a well in it, fill with the egg and yeast mixtures and, with clean hands, gradually incorporate the dry ingredients into the wet until thoroughly combined. Add 35g more flour and knead, adding more flour as necessary, until the dough is formed. Transfer the dough to a work surface and knead for 5 minutes.

4. Oil a medium bowl with rapeseed oil. Form a ball with the dough and place it in the bowl. Cover with cling film and allow the dough to rise until doubled in bulk, 2-3 hours. Knock back the dough, cover and leave to rest for 10 minutes.

5. To form the challah, divide half the dough into 4 equal parts. Rolling with even pressure from the middle to the ends, roll the dough into ropes of equal size. Take all four ropes and pinch them together at the top. Think of the far right strand as no. 1, next as no. 2, then no. 3 and the far left as 4. Move rope 1 between 2 and 3. Pick up 3 and move it where 1 was. Now reverse the count, counting the ropes from the left, 1, 2, 3 and 4. Pick up rope 1 on the left, and move it between the new 2 and 3. Pick up the new rope 3 and move it to where the left rope 1 was. Return to the right and count from the right, as above. Continue braiding by switching back and forth between left and right. Keep braiding until you get to the end. Pinch the ends together and tuck them under the braid. Tuck the top also, if needed. Repeat to braid the remaining half dough. Cover the loaves with cling film and allow to rise until tripled in bulk, about 2 hours. When the loaves have risen sufficiently, the dough will not spring back when poked with a finger.

6. Preheat the oven to 170ºC/gas mark 3. Place an empty baking sheet on the bottom oven rack. Oil two 21.5 x 11.5cm loaf tins.

7. In a small bowl, mix the remaining egg with 2 tablespoons of water. Brush the tops of the loaves with the egg glaze, making sure you get it into the crevices. Place the tins in the oven and immediately pour about 240ml of hot water onto the empty sheet to create steam. Close the oven door immediately and bake until the loaves are golden and make a hollow sound when tapped, about 30 minutes. Turn out onto a rack and cool.

Peshwari Challah

makes 2 x 450g loaves

This savoury challah variation is based on pashwari naan – the Indian bread that's filled with nuts and sultanas. To those good things I've added coconut, spices and a touch of honey. This easily done loaf, partnered with Coconut-Ginger Squash Soup (page 61), also makes a wonderful accompaniment to Indian dishes like Cauliflower Paneer Masala (page 120). It's great as a savoury snack too.

Dough Spices

½ teaspoon ground cumin

¼ teaspoon turmeric

¼ teaspoon ground cardamom

½ teaspoon fennel seed

Filling

40g chopped shelled unsalted pistachios, flaked almonds or raw cashews

35g dessicated coconut

70g sultanas, finely chopped

½ teaspoon cumin

½ teaspoon ground coriander

½ teaspoon kosher salt

½ teaspoon fennel seeds, crushed

3 tablespoons honey

1 medium egg

1. Prepare the challah according to the Classic Challah recipe on page 188 up to Step 4, adding the dough spices to the dry ingredients.

2. Boil a kettle of water. Place the pistachios in a sieve and pour the water over them. Transfer the nuts to a tea towel and roll in the towel to remove their skins.

3. To make the filling, in a mini-food processor, combine the pistachios, coconut, sultanas, cumin, coriander, salt and fennel, and pulse until finely chopped.

4. Cover a baking sheet with baking paper. Halve the dough and roll into a 46 x 23cm rectangle, making the dough thinner at the short ends. Sprinkle half of the nut mixture evenly over the dough and drizzle with the honey. Starting with the nearest long side, roll the dough like a Swiss roll, applying pressure to the ends to taper them slightly. Wind the dough into a spiral, tucking the outmost end underneath the loaf. Place on the baking sheet and cover with cling film. Repeat with the remaining halves of dough and nut mixture, and transfer to the baking sheet. Leave the dough to rise until doubled in bulk, about 2 hours.

5. Preheat the oven to 180ºC/gas mark 4. Place an empty baking sheet in the bottom of the oven and allow it to heat.

6. In a small bowl, combine the egg with 2 tablespoons of water. Brush the risen loaves with the egg glaze, and place in the oven. Pour about 240ml of hot water onto the heated baking sheet to create steam, and immediately close the oven door. Bake until the challah is golden and sounds hollow when tapped, 25-35 minutes. Turn out and cool on a rack.

Chocolate Challah

makes 2 x 450g loaves

Similar to babka but moister, this tempting loaf is delicious when used in a breakfast treat, see Crème Brûlée French Toast (page 152). It's also wonderful on its own as a snack with coffee or milk. Please note that the recipe can be dairy or pareve, depending on the kind of chocolate you use, so please check labels.

1. Prepare the challah according to the Classic Challah recipe (page 188) up to Step 4.

2. Grease two 20.5 x 10cm loaf tins. Combine the chocolate, cinnamon and sugar in a mini food processor, and chop very finely.

3. Halve the dough, and roll one half into a 46 x 23cm rectangle. Sprinkle half the chocolate mixture evenly over the dough and, starting from the nearest long end, roll the dough like a Swiss roll. Bend the roll to form a U shape with the two ends nearest to you. Hold the middle and twist to form a braid with four bumpy sections. Place in one of the prepared tins and, using the tip of a sharp knife, slit each section on the diagonal so the chocolate can be seen. Repeat with the remaining dough half and filling. Cover the loaves with cling film and allow to rise until tripled in bulk, about 2 hours.

4. In a small bowl, combine the egg with 2 tablespoons of water. Brush the risen loaves with the egg glaze, and proceed to bake following the basic Classic Challah recipe.

115g dark chocolate

1 teaspoon cinnamon

100g sugar

1 medium egg

Veal or Beef Stock

makes about 1 litre

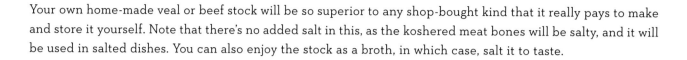

Your own home-made veal or beef stock will be so superior to any shop-bought kind that it really pays to make and store it yourself. Note that there's no added salt in this, as the koshered meat bones will be salty, and it will be used in salted dishes. You can also enjoy the stock as a broth, in which case, salt it to taste.

Geila's Tip

I always double the recipe when making this, and freeze what I don't immediately use for up to eight weeks.

2.7kg veal or beef bones, or a mixture, cut into 5–7cm pieces (ask the butcher to do this)

1 large onion, cut into 1cm dice

150g diced carrots

65g diced celery

1 large leek, trimmed and well cleaned, white part only, cut into 2.5cm lengths

4 tablespoons tomato purée

bouquet garni made with 8 peppercorns, 1 bay leaf, 3 thyme sprigs and 3 crushed garlic cloves, tied in a muslin bag

1. Preheat the oven to 220°C/gas mark 7.

2. In a large roasting tin, arrange the bones in a single layer. Transfer to the oven and roast, until deep brown, about 60 minutes, turning every 20 minutes.

3. Add the onion, carrots, celery and leek to the roasting tin, dot the bones with the tomato purée, and roast for 30 minutes more.

4. Place the bouquet garni in a large stockpot. Transfer the bones and vegetables to the pot. Pour off excess fat from the roasting tin, add 2 cups of water, deglaze the tin, and pour over the bones. (If the tin crust is burned, skip this step.) Add enough cold water to cover the bones by 10cm. Bring to the boil over a high heat, reduce the heat and simmer gently, skimming frequently, until richly flavoured, 5–6 hours. Add more water if the liquid level goes beneath 8cm.

5. Line a colander with muslin and strain the stock through it into a clean pan. Press down on the solids to extract all flavour. Reduce the stock over a medium heat until only about 1 litre remains. Cool and refrigerate. Remove any congealed fat from the surface and use immediately or freeze for up to three weeks.

Best Vegetable Stock

makes about 2 litres

This versatile stock is richly flavourful yet clean tasting – just what you want a vegetable stock to be. In addition to its more traditional uses, I poach fish or chicken in it, or use it to thin soups.

1. In a large pan, heat the oil over a medium heat until hot. Add the onions, celery, carrots, leek and mushrooms, if using, and saute until soft but not brown, stirring occasionally, 10–15 minutes. Stir in the tomato purée and cook until beginning to caramelise, 3–5 minutes. Add the wine and deglaze the pan. Add the bouquet garni and 2 litres of cold water, bring to the boil, reduce the heat and simmer until the vegetables have yielded their flavour, 30–40 minutes.

2. Line a large sieve with muslin and strain the stock through it. Press down on the solids to extract more flavour. Use immediately, refrigerate for up to 3 days or freeze for up to 6 weeks.

1½ tablespoon extra-virgin olive oil

450g onions, roughly chopped

100g diced celery

100g diced carrots

1 large leek, trimmed and well cleaned, white part only, cut into 2.5cm lengths

225g roughly chopped mushrooms (optional)

2 tablespoon tomato purée

120ml dry white wine

bouquet garni made with 8 peppercorns, 1 bay leaf, 2 thyme sprigs and 1 crushed garlic clove, tied in a muslin bag

Crêpes

makes 16

Every cook should have a crêpe recipe up his or her sleeve. These traditional French pancakes are the basis of a wide range of sweet and savoury recipes, like blintzes on page 159, or dishes for which they're filled with cheese or vegetables. This version is cook-friendly; make them once, and subsequent batches will be child's play.

1. In a large measuring jug, combine the flour, eggs, sugar, if using, butter and milk. Using a hand blender, blend until smooth. Alternatively, blend in an ordinary blender. Refrigerate for at least 60 minutes.

2. Heat a crêpe pan or small frying pan over a medium heat. Spray the pan with non-stick cooking spray and wipe it out with kitchen paper. Pour 120ml of batter into the middle of the pan, and tilt the pan from side to side to coat the bottom evenly. When the edges of the crêpe begin to brown, after 1–2 minutes, flip it in the pan, or use your fingers to turn it over. If necessary, first loosen the crêpe around the edge with the tip of a small knife.

3. Cook for 30 seconds on the second side, transfer the crêpe to a plate and cover with baking paper. Repeat with the remaining batter.

130g plain flour

2 medium eggs

2 tablespoons sugar, if making a dessert dish

2 tablespoons melted unsalted butter

240ml milk

Paneer

makes about 450g

Paneer, a staple of Indian cooking, is a fresh, curd cheese, similar to cottage cheese but more compact. Cubed, it adds a welcome cool creaminess to spicy dishes, like Cauliflower Paneer Masala on page 120. I've yet to find a kosher version, but it's really easy to make at home, and stores well in a water bath in the fridge. You might want to involve your kids in the process as it provides a great introduction to cheese making.

---

1. In a large pan, heat the milk over a medium heat to a temperature of 82ºC. Turn off the heat and begin to stir in the lemon juice, 1 tablespoon at a time. Watch carefully. Stop adding the juice as soon as the milk separates into curds and whey. Add the salt and leave to stand until cool enough to handle, about 30 minutes.

2. Line a colander or large sieve with muslin. Strain the milk and rinse the curds under cold water to remove excess lemon juice. Twist the muslin to eliminate liquid. While still in the muslin, press the curds into a square, and transfer the square in the muslin to a plate. Place a chopping board on it and weight it with a tin to further drain and firm the paneer for at least 1 hour.

3. Meanwhile, fill a bowl large enough to accommodate the paneer with water and add ice cubes. Place the paneer in the water, transfer to the fridge and chill for at least 1 hour or overnight. (To store the paneer longer, drain it and return it to the fridge in a fresh water bath for up to 4 weeks.) Remove the paneer, drain, pat dry, and cut as your recipe directs.

3.8 litres milk

juice from 2 lemons (about 6 tablespoons)

1 teaspoon kosher salt

Béchamel Two Ways

makes about 0.5 litres

Soya milk gives the pareve version of this traditional cream sauce, a kitchen basic, and has all the creamy richness of the dairy kind. Use milk plus double cream to make the dairy version particularly rich.

Convert It

To make this pareve, substitute margarine for the butter and unsweetened soya milk or unsweetened coconut milk for the milk, or milk and cream respectively.

4 tablespoons unsalted butter

6 tablespoons plain flour

480ml hot milk or 300ml milk plus 180ml double cream

½ teaspoon salt, or more, to taste

⅛ teaspoon nutmeg (optional)

1. In a medium saucepan, melt the butter over a medium heat. When the foaming subsides, add the flour, mix well, and allow to bubble for 1-2 minutes. Whisk in the milk gradually, continuing to whisk until the mixture is smooth and has the consistency of sour cream. If a thicker béchamel is called for, continue to cook until the desired consistency.

2. Add the salt and nutmeg, if using, and stir.

Sun-dried Tomato and Herb Dressing

makes about 250ml

Herb dressings are a 'modern' approach to providing big flavour quickly. Just brush this savoury example over grilled meat or chicken, or spoon it over crusty bread. See page 100 for another dressing recipe.

150g sun-dried tomatoes in oil

120ml extra-virgin olive oil

4 tablespoons fresh oregano leaves

2 garlic cloves

¼ teaspoon chilli flakes, or to taste

8 fresh basil leaves

In a food processor, combine the tomatoes, olive oil, oregano, garlic, chilli flakes and basil, and pulse until the mixture is well chopped, but be careful not to over-chop it into a paste. Use immediately or refrigerate for up to one week.

Mayonnaise with Variations
makes about 250ml

Unlike the shop-bought kind, home-made mayonnaise is richly flavoured – and it's prepared in an instant. You can make it by hand using a whisk or hand blender, or in an electric blender. Make sure all your ingredients and utensils are at room temperature before you begin.

1. Combine the oils in a large measuring jug.

2. In a medium non-porous bowl, the bowl of a stand mixer or in a blender, combine the yolks, mustard, if using, and salt. Whisk or beat until the yolks begin to get sticky, 1–2 minutes. Beating constantly, begin to incorporate the oils, starting drop by drop and increasing the flow as the mixture stiffens. After 240ml of the oil has been added, add the lemon juice or vinegar. Add the remaining oil as before and adjust the seasoning. Serve immediately or refrigerate for up to five days.

Geila's Tips

To warm the bowl in which the mayo is made, I fill it with hot water, drain the water and dry the bowl. Then I add the yolks, which come to room temperature 'automatically' in the hot bowl.

180ml extra-virgin olive oil

180ml rapeseed oil

3 large egg yolks

2 teaspoons Dijon mustard, or ½ teaspoon mustard powder (optional)

1 teaspoon kosher salt, plus more, if needed

1½ tablespoons lemon juice or white wine vinegar

Red Pepper Mayonnaise
makes about 250ml

1. On the hob or under the grill, roast the peppers until the skin is uniformly charred. Place the peppers in a paper bag or bowl. Close the bag or cover the bowl. Allow the peppers to steam until they become cool enough to handle. Remove the stems, skin and seeds, transfer to a blender or food processor and purée, or use a hand blender.

2. Meanwhile, transfer the mayonnaise to a medium bowl. Mix in the pepper purée and serve immediately or refrigerate for up to five days.

2 red peppers

250ml mayonnaise

Wasabi Mayonnaise
makes about 250ml

In a small bowl, combine the wasabi and 2 tablespoons of water. Beat in the mayonnaise. Serve immediately or refrigerate for up to five days.

1 tablespoon wasabi powder

250ml mayonnaise

The Chart:
Ingredient Exchanges at a Glance

Exchanges For Kosher Foods

For Dairy Dishes	For Pareve Dishes	For Meat Dishes
Butter	Almond oil Rapeseed oil + salt Coconut oil Grapeseed oil Hazelnut oil Margarine	*In Order of Preference* Grapeseed oil Rapeseed oil Olive oil Duck fat Chicken fat Margarine
Cheese Grated Parmesan	Non-dairy cheeses are not recommended Toasted ground pine nuts + breadcrumbs + salt (page 124)	Non-dairy cheeses are not recommended Toasted ground pine nuts + breadcrumbs + salt (page 124)
Cream	Coconut milk MimicCreme MimicCreme Healthy Top (page 17)	Velouté sauce (stock + roux) MimicCreme MimicCreme Healthy Top (page 17)

For Dairy Dishes	For Pareve Dishes	For Meat Dishes
Milk	Almond milk Coconut milk Hazelnut milk Rice milk Soya milk Vegetable stock (page 193)	Almond milk Coconut milk Hazelnut milk Rice milk Soya milk Vegetable stock (page 193) Chicken stock
Stocks Vegetable stock (page 193) G. Washington's Golden Seasoning Broth (page 18) Fish stock	Vegetable stock (page 193) G. Washington's Golden Seasoning Broth (page 18) Fish stock	Chicken stock Beef stock (page 192) Veal stock (page 192)

For Non-Kosher Foods

Meat and Shellfish	
Bacon	Duck prosciutto (page 24) or duck pastrami, sliced and fried
Crab	Surimi crab (page 19)
Minced Pork	Minced veal + minced turkey
Ham	Smoked Dark Meat Turkey (page 19)
Lobster, mussels, scallops	Any firm, fatty fish, such as sea bass or salmon
Pork Chops	Veal chops
Prawns	Konnyaku prawn (page 19) Surimi prawn (page 19)

For Passover

Breadcrumbs	Ground matzo Matzo meal/matzo crumbs
Cornflour	Potato starch
Icing Sugar, 140g	Kosher for Passover icing sugar 200g granulated sugar + 1 tablespoon potato starch, pulsed in a food processor until powdery
Corn Syrup, 250ml	250ml granulated sugar + 80ml water, boiled
Flour, 130g	For baking, 65g fine matzo meal + 25g potato starch

Sources

Many kosher ingredients can be found at www.amazon.co.uk and www.ocado.com, as well as kosher ingredient sites including www.justkosher.co.uk, www.rakusens.co.uk and www.kosherfoodonline.eu. Also check health food sites, www.goodnessdirect.co.uk and vegan food sites, www.veganvillage.co.uk.

For recommended brands, see The Store Cupboard (page 17).

Black Soy Beans with Salt
www.amazon.co.uk

Barbary Duck Breast
www.fishfanatics.co.uk

Breadcrumbs
www.yardenoutlet.co.uk

Cheeses

Cheddar
www.goodnessdirect.co.uk

Parmesan-Reggiano
www.artisanpantry.com

Mozzarella
www.goodnessdirect.co.uk

Leicester
www.coombecastle.com

Other Cheeses
www.justkosher.co.uk
www.buteisland.com

Chestnuts
www.kosherfoodonline.eu

Chicken Stock
www.kosherfoodonline.eu

Chocolate
www.rumplers.co.uk
www.thenutfreechocolatecompany.co.uk
www.kosherfoodonline.eu
www.chocdock.co.uk
www.yardenoutlet.co.uk

Crème Fraîche
www.kosherfoodonline.eu

Extracts
www.lheo.co.uk
www.amazon.co.uk

Food Colourings
www.rumplers.co.uk
www.amazon.co.uk
www.cakescookiesandcraftsshop.co.uk

G. Washingon's Golden Seasoning Broth
www.amazon.com

Konnyaku
www.japanesefoodshop.co.uk

Mascarpone
www.artisanpantry.com

Meat
www.kosherdeli.co.uk

Miso and Mirin
www.clearspring.co.uk

Non-Dairy Cream
www.alprosoya.co.uk

Noodles
www.yardenoutlet.co.uk

Nut Milks
www.goodnessdirect.co.uk

Panko
www.kikkoman.co.uk
www.japanesekitchen.co.uk

Praline Paste
www.infusions4chefs.co.uk

Ramen
www.clearspring.co.uk

Rapeseed Oil, Extra-Virgin Olive Oil,
Grapeseed Oil
www.justkosher.co.uk
www.yardenoutlet.co.uk

Rendered Chicken Fat
www.justkosher.co.uk

Rendered Duck Fat
www.justkosher.co.uk

Sausages
www.justkosher.co.uk

Sake
www.kosherwine.com

Sea Salt
www.clearspring.co.uk

Smoked Dark Meat Turkey
ww.kosherdeli.co.uk

Soya Milk
www.alprosoya.co.uk

Surimi
find the Dyna-sea or Fjord brand
at your local supermarket

Toasted Sesame Oil
www.clearspring.co.uk

White Truffle Oil
www.amazon.co.uk

Wonton Wrappers
www.theasiancookshop.co.uk

Index

Index

Index

Index

Acknowledgements

Both authors would like to thank Kyle Cathie and their US publisher and editor, Anja Schmidt. Her even-tempered, warmly attentive professionalism has made working with her a joy. Great gratitude also to our agent, Stéphanie Abou of Foundry Media, for her faith in the book and continued support. And many thanks to Antonis Achilleos for his wonderful photos.

Geila Hocherman
First and foremost I would like to thank Arthur Boehm, who, after 25 years of friendship, gave his blessing, support, talent and blood, sweat and tears to help me realise this book. Arthur, you are my voice, and without your words and skill I would never have got this far. Writing this book has been a joy both personally and professionally. You have spoiled me for anyone else.

I would also like to thank Sheila Schlussel, Ron Miguel, Ann Avidor, Ilene Aronson, Ellen Breslow-Newhouse and Deborah Zimbler for their generosity and cooking companionship over the years. They are always available, offering recipes, culinary discourse, advice and friendship all at the same time.

The support I've received from David Strah, Barry Miguel, Nomi Stolzenberg-Myers, Ruth Rifkin, Caroline Migliore, Joan Schulik, Kim Amzallag and Susan Shay has been nothing short of extraordinary. Their unwavering faith in me and enthusiasm for the book has really carried the day.

I always wondered why people would joke about the need to be extra-friendly to their butcher. Now I know why! Thanks to Paul Whitman of Fischer Brothers and Leslie in Manhattan for elevating my kosher meat standards. Thanks also to my good and loving friend/personal photographer Yvette Pomerantz and to my 'lawyer on demand', Max Leitman. And a big thanks to Renee Green for pulling me over the pond and generously giving a new friend such great support.

Lastly, I would like to thank my family. It's rare to have such pure love and devotion as they've given me. The unending support of my parents, Moshe and Allie Hocherman, has given me the freedom to pursue this project, whether by providing professional grandparent service, chauffeuring or listening: they have been with me every step of the way. Ditto for my brother Adam, whose flirtations with the vegan lifestyle helped me to discover new cooking possibilities. Most of all, thank you to my magnificent daughter Tess – for recipe inspiration, for your advice and opinions, which reflect your particularly sensitive palate, and most of all, for your patience. Your encouragement gave me permission to do the book in the first place. You'll never know how much that means to me.

Arthur Boehm
Thanks first to Geila Hocherman, dear friend and now co-author. Working with her and writing about her marvellous food has deepened my devotion to her, as well as being a great pleasure. I thank her also for putting me in touch with my inner balabusta.

Thanks also to my friends Del Flynn, Jinx Gingold, John Kane and Tama Starr for caring and support. And several big licks to my cats, Chee-Chee and Poulenc.